It's Our World, Too!

J
302
Hoo
Hoose
It's our world, too!

R615123
12.95

DATE DUE			

BL

It's Our World, Too!

STORIES OF YOUNG PEOPLE WHO ARE MAKING A DIFFERENCE

BY PHILLIP HOOSE

LITTLE, BROWN AND COMPANY

BOSTON TORONTO LONDON

Title page photograph: Young people from war-torn countries around the world, members of Children of War.

Copyright © 1993 by Phillip Hoose

First Edition

Library of Congress Cataloging-in-Publication Data

Hoose, Phillip M., 1947–
    It's our world, too! : stories of young people who are making a
difference / by Phillip Hoose. — 1st ed.
        p.   cm.
    ISBN 0-316-37241-2
    1. Children as volunteers — United States — Juvenile literature.
2. Social action — United States — Juvenile literature.   3. Community
development — United States — Citizen participation — Juvenile
literature.   I. Title.
HQ784.V64H65   1993
302'.14 — dc20   92-24873

Joy Street Books are published by Little, Brown and Company (Inc.)

10   9   8   7   6   5   4   3   2   1

HAWK

Published simultaneously in Canada
by Little, Brown & Company (Canada) Limited

Printed in the U.S.A.

I'd like to thank the many young people who let me interview them.

Thanks, too, to the students in Val Vasser's class at Fred P. Hall School and Cheryl Nolan's class at Breakwater School for allowing me to read chapters to them, to Jena Ullman and Toby Prosky for reviewing chapters, and to Ted DeMille for helping me with the handbook section. Thanks to the fifth-graders of Nick Byrne's class at the Tenakill School in Closter, to Cheryl Nolan, and to Edhorah Frazier for commenting on the proposal for this book.

The following people helped me find young activists to interview: A. T. Birmingham-Young of the Giraffe Project; Nancy Leonard of the Jefferson Foundation; musicians Sally Rogers, Danny Einbender, and Nancy Schimmel; Judith Webb of Young and Teen Peacemakers; Arnie Alpert of the American Friends Service Committee; Judith Thompson of Children of War; Kathleen Kirby of the Constitutional Rights Foundation; Ray Santiago of the Funding Exchange; Ann Brown of the Rural Organizing and Cultural Center in Lexington, Mississippi; Mary Ruthstotler of the National Women's History Project; Charlotte Villareal; Gail Brooks; Andrew Frost; Razel Solow; and Joseph Pupello; and Eha Kern and Camy Condon helped me arrange interviews.

Dr. Arthur Young, Dr. Howard Zinn, and Dr. Charles Blockson helped me find information about young activists in history.

Thanks to Dr. Harold Hackett, Dr. Sharon Kinsman, Ree Scheck, Eileen O'Brien, Donna Halvorsen, Kim Harris, David Lieber, and Todd Putnam for helping me find photographs and other information.

Phyllis Wender and Susie Perlman helped this book find a publisher. Melanie Kroupa, my editor, helped me make it as good as it could be.

Biggest thanks of all to my wife, Shoshana. This book was our idea together, and we spent many exciting hours thinking about its potential. Without her, it wouldn't be here. And thanks to Hannah Hoose — a fine young editor, caring activist, and special friend — and Ruby Hoose, who toddled up the stairs and into my office to keep me from working all the time.

THANK-YOU

CONTENTS

PREFACE

I first heard the words "It's our world, too!" from Paul Gravelle, of Winterport, Maine. He told me a story about the Sunday morning a few years before, when he had been walking out of church. Just outside the door, people had been signing petitions to stop the spread of nuclear weapons.

Paul was eleven at the time, and very worried about such weapons. He asked if he could sign, too. The worker smiled at him and told him he was too young.

Paul was puzzled. Why shouldn't he be able to sign? Did anyone really think that if nuclear bombs ever got dropped, they would kill only adults? By the time Paul reached the car, he had an idea. "I'll write a petition for kids," he told his mother. "It's our world, too!"

The same evening, Paul wrote out a young people's peace petition and began to pass it among his friends. In turn, they passed it to their friends. It has attracted over twenty-four thousand signatures from kids in all fifty states and in twelve nations.

During the past year, I interviewed many young people ages eight to seventeen who, like Paul, have taken steps to change the world for the better. When asked why, many said the same thing: it's our world, too.

They were a diverse group: rich, poor, middle class. Some had two parents, some one; a few grew up without parents at all. Their ancestors came from Europe, Africa, Mexico, Cambodia, the Philippines. One group lives in Sweden. But they had important things in common. They cared about others. They were willing to take risks. They didn't give up easily. They were unchanging in their principles but adaptable in their tactics: if one thing didn't work, they tried something else.

Above all, they believed they had power *now,* even though they couldn't vote yet and still lived under someone else's roof. In fact, some said they thought they had *more* power now than they would have when they were older — that as young people they had special advantages. Among them were:

Energy. "While you're young, you have energy," said Caitlin Chestnut, a fourteen-year-old peace activist from New Mexico. "Adults get tired. Kids bounce back more quickly."

Time. They believed they had more time now for projects than they would when they had to support themselves and take care of family members.

A clear sense of right and wrong. "Someone told me that when I got older, I'd be less idealistic," said Alex Reinert, a seventeen-year-old student activist. "Even if that's true, right now we have a powerful vision of what we think the world should be. We shouldn't ignore it or let ourselves be put down as idealistic. When you're young, you have a special ability to think about things that have been accepted for a thousand years and say, 'We have to stop that.' "

The power of being underestimated by adults. "Sometimes the media will respond to a call from young people just because they seem surprised that we're actually doing something," says Michael Brown, sixteen, who started a community garden in rural Mississippi.

School: the perfect place to organize. The kids in these stories organized and planned in rest rooms, around lockers, on the bus going home, and on the playground. They were able to take advantage of official meeting rooms, photocopy machines, adult sponsors, and their schools' communication systems. And of course they gained strength from the biggest advantage of all: each other.

This book is a guide to power for young people. It is designed to offer examples and tactics that can help you change your life, school, neighborhood, town, city, environment, or world for the better.

Though your generation is facing some new and very hard challenges — who else but you ever grew up beneath a hole in the sky? — there's plenty you can do. In this book, you'll meet people your age who are leading the way to important changes. You can gain from their courage, caring, and shrewdness, and then take your own steps to change things for the better. They're right: you may be young, but it *is* your world, too.

Kids plan statue to world peace

How Youths Rallied To Dolphins' Cause

Teen honored for stand against gangs

South Florida students help preserve rain forests

Young doers teach indifferent adults

9-year-old sees results of his fight with city hall

Student talks tough about gangs

Kids-for-peace submit 21,000 calls to disarm

It's Our World, Too!

A HISTORY

It was newsies such as these who brought down the two biggest newspaper owners in the United States.

YOUNG ACTIVISTS WHO WENT BEFORE YOU

You may not know it, but young activists helped win America's independence, end slavery, secure better conditions for workers, and win civil rights for all Americans. In most history books, you never hear about them. "We're not taught about younger people who have made a difference," says Sarah Rosen, fourteen, who led a demonstration for women's rights at her school when she was ten. "So studying history almost makes you feel like you're not a real person."

Before you read about kids who are working for peace and justice today, take a look at a few who went before you.

CHILDREN OF INDEPENDENCE

Ebeneezer Fox was a fifteen-year-old apprentice barber in 1779 when he heard a man in a crowded Boston street singing:

> *All you that have bad masters,*
> *And cannot get your due;*
> *Come, come, my brave boys,*
> *And join with our ship's crew.*

Nobody could have better described the way Ebeneezer felt. And there were tens of thousands of apprentices in Colonial cities who felt the same way. They were boys, usually between the ages of ten and seventeen, whose fathers signed a contract for them to live with a master tradesman, such as a watchmaker, leather tanner, or shoemaker, for seven years.

Most boys hated their apprenticeships. They got no pay at all for seven years. Often they were treated like servants, doing chores around their masters' houses and land. Sometimes they were beaten. Often the master didn't teach them the trade until the very end of the contract, and then only for fear that the apprentice would run away.

When the Colonies began agitating for independence in the 1760s and 1770s, many boys like Ebeneezer Fox organized and fought against Great Britain.

They dreamed that in a new nation of free citizens, they, too, would be independent — not only from the British but from their masters as well. They compared themselves to the Colonies and their masters to King George III of England. Ebeneezer wrote in his journal:

> I and other boys situated similarly to myself, thought . . . it was our duty and our privilege to assert our own rights. . . . I was doing myself a great injustice by remaining in bondayge, when I ought to go free; and that the time was come when I should liberate myself from the thraldom of others.

While Ebeneezer and other apprentices left their masters to battle British soldiers, girls fought for independence, too. They joined their mothers in "patriotic sewing circles," spinning cloth as fast as they could to make up for the cloth they now refused to buy from the British. "As I am (as we say) a daughter of liberty I chuse to wear as much of my own manufactory as possible," wrote twelve-year-old Anna Winslow of Boston in 1772.

The girls knew their quick fingers were just as important to liberty as were the fingers wrapped around muskets and bayonets. Charity Clark, fifteen, who spun wool from her home in New York City, wrote to her British cousin that freedom would be won not only by soldiers, but by "a fighting army of amazones [strong women] . . . armed with spinning wheels."

YOUNG FIGHTERS FOR BETTER WORKING CONDITIONS

In the fall of 1790, nine young boys — the oldest was twelve — from poor families in Rhode Island became the first factory workers in American history. They had been

▲ ▲ ● ▬▬▬

"ONE GIRL AT THE MANCHESTER MILL, FULLY ASSISTED BY MACHINERY, PRODUCES AS MUCH VALUE AS EIGHT LABORERS IN OUR FIELD."
— LETTER IN A NEW ENGLAND NEWSPAPER, 1819

▬▬▬ ● ■ ■

4

hired to work in a textile mill, using newly invented machinery to turn yarn into cotton. They were the first of a great tide of child laborers.

By 1830, more than a million children worked in textile mills. Many worked from dawn till dusk every day but Sunday. They made perhaps a dollar a week, which they turned over to their parents. Their only holidays were Christmas, Easter, and a half day for the Fourth of July.

In the 1830s, children began to fight for their rights by joining and leading dozens of strikes for more pay and shorter hours. Eleven-year-old Harriet Hanson was one of 1,500 girls who walked out of a giant textile mill in Lowell, Massachusetts, in 1836 to protest the company's plan to raise the fees they had to pay to sleep in a company-owned boarding house.

On the day of the strike, while the girls on the upper floors walked out of the mill singing, the girls on Harriet's floor hesitated. They began to whisper. What if they lost their jobs? What would the company do to them?

Harriet was disgusted. "What do we have to lose?" she asked. Still, they stood indecisively at their looms. "I don't care what you do," she said finally. "I am going to turn out whether anyone else does or not."

Eyes straight ahead, Harriet turned around and marched toward the door. In the next moment, she heard a great shuffling of feet. She looked back to see the entire floor lining up behind her. Harriet never forgot her moment of decision. "As I looked back on the long line that followed me," she later wrote, "I was more proud than I have ever been since."

Strike leader Harriet Hanson at age eighteen.

▲ ▲ ● ▬▬▬▬

"I NEVER CARED MUCH FOR MACHINERY. IN SWEET JUNE WEATHER I WOULD LEAN FAR OUT THE WINDOW, AND TRY NOT TO HEAR THE UNCEASING CLASH OF SOUND INSIDE."
— A LOWELL FACTORY GIRL

▬▬▬▬ ● ■ ■

YOUNG CONDUCTORS ON THE UNDERGROUND RAILROAD

The first black children to live in America had been snatched from their homes in Africa, chained, and thrown into the bottoms of crowded ships for a long, stormy voyage across the Atlantic. Many died on the way.

Those who survived were sold to plantation owners.

5

They were measured and weighed and auctioned as if they were cattle or sheep. They became part of their white master's property, along with his furniture and crops and land.

Black babies were often separated from their parents to prevent love within families from threatening the masters' control. Boys and girls were made to do hard work in the fields and around the plantation house from the time they were very young. They were not allowed to learn to read or write. They were often whipped.

Between 1820 and 1860, thousands of slaves fled the South into the free Northern states and all the way to Canada in a long relay chain of secret houses called the Underground Railroad. There was no map; a runaway slave learned the path one station, as the houses were called, at a time. The runaways were tracked like animals by hunters on horseback, who received a bounty, or reward, for every escaped slave they caught.

Since the bounty hunters paid closest attention to adults, it was often up to the children of families on the Underground Railroad to act as "conductors" — to look out for runaway slaves and hide them before the slave catchers could capture them.

In the 1820s, a young Quaker boy named Allen Jay lived in an Underground Railroad station in southern Indiana. Whenever runaway slaves appeared, Allen ran out from his hiding place in a peach orchard and hustled them to safety, conducting them through the peach trees and on into a cornfield, where they would run crouching between tall rows of corn until they reached the base of a big walnut tree. There he would tell the fugitive to rest until he could return with a basket of food.

Once it was dark, Allen would harness his parents' horse to a wagon full of straw, which he heaped over the runaway. Then he would drive five miles north to the next station — his grandfather's house.

Lucinda Wilson was another young conductor. She lived in southern Ohio. Like Allen, it was her job to look out for runaways and help them. One morning when she was thirteen, a movement caught her eye while she was picking berries in a field near her house. She saw two young runaway girls hiding at the edge of the field. As she walked closer, she could see they were exhausted, their bare feet swollen and bleeding.

She helped them back to her home and began to fix them a meal while they lay down. Suddenly there was a heavy knock on the door. Quickly Lucinda pulled the girls up the stairs to her room. She helped push one girl into a clothes hamper. She gave the other a set of her nightclothes, and the two leapt into bed together, the runaway hiding her face inside Lucinda's nightcap.

Instantly they heard boot steps on the stairs. Two bounty hunters burst open the door to Lucinda's room, but all they could see were two girls sleeping soundly. They left quickly, apologizing as they retreated. Months later, Lucinda learned that the two girls had arrived safely — and free — in Canada.

"WE WANT TO GO TO SCHOOL."

After the Civil War, in which many men were killed or injured, even more children went to work to help their families. By 1900, more than two million American kids were

Young workers in a Pennsylvania mine, 1909. Many boys died before they reached manhood.

working in mines and mills, barns and fields, stables and sweatshops. In the coal mines of Pennsylvania, boys as young as nine were harnessed like mules to wagons of coal, which they were ordered to pull down into the earth and then back up full of coal. Factories were filled with new machinery that was especially dangerous to small workers. "Once in a while a hand gets mashed, or a foot," explained one factory owner to an investigator. "But it doesn't amount to anything."

Children fought back. In Paterson, New Jersey, kids walked out of their factory when the company suddenly delayed their lunch break from noon to one, for even by noon their stomachs were growling. They won. In Philadelphia, children who worked sixty hours a week in textile mills went on strike, carrying signs that read, "We want to go to school!" They, too, won a shorter week.

In 1899, a group of determined young boys from New York City took on two of the richest and most powerful men in America. William Randolph Hearst and Joseph Pulitzer owned the two biggest newspapers in New York. These two giants were used to getting their own way simply by rolling over people.

Many newsies started working in New York City when they were very young.

In those days, the papers were delivered to buyers by newsboys, or "newsies," who bought the papers from the company and then sold them to readers for a little more money, keeping the difference.

The trouble started when Hearst and Pulitzer decided to raise the price that the newsies had to pay for their papers. They didn't figure kids could do anything about it. But the newsies were used to scrapping on the streets of America's toughest city. They quickly formed a union and announced that they would refuse to deliver the Hearst and Pulitzer papers until their buying price returned to normal. "We're here for our rights and we will die defendin' 'em," explained one ten-year-old striker named Boots McAleenan.

The newsies demonstrated at the places where delivery carts usually gave them their bundles of papers. They put signs up on nearby lampposts saying, "Help the Newsboys" and "Our Cause Is Just." Hundreds of boys surrounded the carts and shouted at the drivers, who quickly tossed the papers over the side and fled.

As newspaper sales plummeted, advertisers began to ask for their money back. When sales dropped by two-thirds, Hearst and Pulitzer gave up. They offered a deal that gave the newsies even more money than before. The newsies snapped up the deal and went back to selling papers.

It took until 1938 for the nation to outlaw child labor. Even now there are many kids who work too long and hard, especially picking crops. But were it not for the courage of thousands of young people like Harriet Hanson and the newsies — and the adults who helped them — the situation would almost certainly be much worse.

YOUNG FIGHTERS FOR CIVIL RIGHTS

Every Martin Luther King Day, students hear how black Americans in the 1950s and 1960s overcame laws that split society into two groups: black and white. But while we hear about Dr. King and Rosa Parks, we rarely hear about the thousands of young activists who joined the fight for freedom.

In the fall of 1957, armed soldiers escorted nine black students to Little Rock Central High School. Once they got inside, they were on their own.

In 1954, the U.S. Supreme Court ruled that there could no longer be separate schools for black and white children. The decision angered many whites. Black children had to face that anger when they walked through the doors of southern schools for the first time.

One such child was fifteen-year-old Elizabeth Eckford. On September 4, 1957, she tried to become the first black student ever to enter Central High School in Little Rock, Arkansas. Actually Elizabeth was one of nine black students who had signed up to enroll that day. Expecting trouble, they had agreed to travel to school together. But at the last minute, the pickup place got changed. Elizabeth didn't have a phone, so she didn't get word.

She put on the new dress she had made for the first day of school and waited for her ride to arrive. When no one came, she picked up her notebook and walked nervously out her front door alone.

Soon Elizabeth could see that a mob of white people, held back by police, had formed across the street from her school. A line of Arkansas National Guardsmen, carrying rifles with bayonets, blocked the entrance to the school. At first Elizabeth thought they were there to protect her from the mob. Terrified, she tried to pass through the soldiers and get into the building. But they pointed their bayonets at her and blocked her way. They would let only white students through.

There was nowhere to run and no one to help her. She made her way to a bench by the bus stop at the end of the block as the screaming mob broke past the police and surrounded her. Several screamed of lynching her. After what seemed like forever, the bus appeared and a sympathetic woman guided Elizabeth aboard. Later that fall, it took one thousand federal troops to protect Elizabeth and the other five black girls and three boys so they could enroll at Central High.

But there were no soldiers to protect them once they got inside the building. All year long they were taunted and tripped, scalded in the showers, ignored, and called names. "After a while," recalled Melba Patillo Beals, one of the nine students, "I started saying to myself, 'Am I less than human? Why are they doing this? What's wrong with me?' "

But Melba, Elizabeth, and the other seven had the courage to stay all year at Central High. Ernest Green, the only senior in the group, became the first black student ever to receive a diploma there.

By 1960, young people were sitting in at lunch counters, kneeling in at churches and wading in at beaches and pools throughout the South in order to integrate all-white facilities. College students rode into the heart of the segregationist South to try to integrate bus stations. They were beaten, threatened, spat upon, and jailed. Several were killed.

In 1963, an army of young people — many in early grade school — turned the tide in one of the most important episodes of the civil rights movement. The scene was Birmingham, Alabama, which Martin Luther King, Jr., called the hardest city in the U.S. for blacks to live in. That spring, Dr. King and other civil rights leaders thought up a dramatic idea to try to force Birmingham's white leaders to integrate the city's downtown stores. They decided to march on the

▲ ▲ ● ■

"IT IS DIFFICULT TO EXAGGERATE THE CREATIVE CONTRIBUTION OF YOUNG NEGROES. THEY TOOK NONVIOLENT RESISTANCE . . . AND DEVELOPED ORIGINAL FORMS OF APPLICATION — SIT-INS, FREEDOM RIDES, AND WADE-INS. TO ACCOMPLISH THIS, THEY FIRST TRANSFORMED THEMSELVES."
— DR. MARTIN LUTHER KING, JR.

■ ● ■ ■

stores every single day. They knew the police would be sure to haul the marchers off to jail. The idea was to fill up the Birmingham jails with so many demonstrators that police would have no place to put other protestors.

Every day, more and more demonstrators were locked up. But before long, all the adults who were willing to go to jail were behind bars. One night when Dr. King asked for new volunteers to be arrested, only a handful of adults stood up.

But Dr. King noticed that a group of young people was standing, too. Some appeared to be third- and fourth-graders. At first Dr. King told them they were too young. But as the days passed and adult volunteers became even harder to find, he made the decision to let them join in.

On the morning of May 2, 1963, nearly one thousand children marched out of the Sixteenth Street Baptist Church and into the streets of Birmingham, carrying signs and chanting for freedom. Some were only six years old.

Police began to arrest them by the dozens. Singing, the children climbed into the police wagons. Soon the police ran out of wagons. Then they ran out of police cars. Then fire trucks. By nightfall, six hundred kids were in jail. "I have been inspired and moved today," Dr. King told their parents at a rally that evening. "I have never seen anything like it."

Word spread around the country. The next morning, dozens of reporters and photographers flew into the Birmingham airport. Just before noon, sixty more children walked out of the church and into the streets. The police were waiting. They knew the nation had seen children make them look foolish the night before on TV. This time they were determined to keep the kids away from the downtown business section without making arrests.

As the children approached, police aimed special fire hoses called monitor guns at them. A command was given, and a blast of water struck the young protestors like a truck, knocking them backward. Still holding on to each other, they tried to keep singing a song called "Freedom." As a

▲ ▲ ● ■■■■

"IN JAIL THESE CHILDREN, THESE TEENAGERS, THESE YOUNG WOMEN AND MEN SANG AND PRAYED AND REFUSED TO DESERT ONE ANOTHER. EVENTUALLY, THEIR COURAGE AND DETERMINATION — AND BLOOD — FORCED THEIR GOVERNMENT TO DEFEND DEMOCRACY, MADE IT POSSIBLE FOR EVERYONE IN AMERICA TO HAVE THE FREEDOM TO RIDE, TO SIT, TO EAT, TO GO TO THE REST ROOM, JUST ABOUT WHEREVER THEY WANTED TO."
— VINCENT HARDING, HOPE AND HISTORY

■■■■ ● ■ ■

12

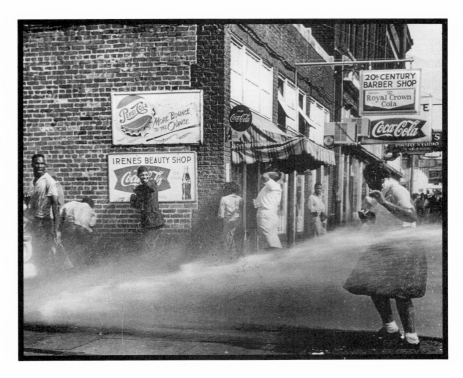

Birmingham, Alabama, police blast a group of brave young civil rights demonstrators with powerful water hoses.

horrified crowd watched, the police walked forward, increasing the pressure.

Meanwhile, hundreds of other young people poured out of the church and began running for the downtown area. Police let dogs loose to chase them. One newspaper photographer took a picture of a young black boy being bitten in the stomach by a police dog. Millions of people who saw the picture the next day were at once inspired by the boy's courage and horrified by the police action. Overnight, the children of Birmingham had created a pressure of public opinion that was even stronger than the force of the fire hoses that had been used against them, and within weeks, an agreement was made between black and white leaders in Birmingham that ended segregation in the city.

A VOYAGER FOR PEACE

Young people have tried hard to ensure world peace, too. One young girl from Maine helped to thaw the ice of the Cold War between the United States and the Soviet Union.

13

In the winter of 1982, ten-year-old Samantha Smith wrote a letter to the leader of the Soviet Union, Yuri Andropov. Samantha had become worried about nuclear weapons after watching a TV show.

In her letter, she got right to the point: "Are you going to have a war or not?" she asked Andropov. "If you are not, please tell me how you are going to help not have a war."

She stuck on forty cents' postage and asked her dad to mail it on the way to work. Five months later she received Andropov's reply: "I invite you, if your parents will let you, to come to our country, the best time being the summer . . . and see for yourself: in the Soviet Union — everyone is for peace and friendship among peoples."

Samantha Smith's visit was filmed and written about by journalists from around the world. Through their cameras, adults saw Samantha laughing in Moscow, swimming at a children's summer camp on the Black Sea, and riding a bicycle in Leningrad. The children around her didn't seem like monsters; they seemed just like children everywhere.

During her visit, Samantha made deep friendships. "Sometimes at night we talked about peace," she wrote. "None of them hated America and none of them ever wanted war. It seemed strange even to talk about war when we all got along so well together."

By the time Samantha Smith got home, all her old questions had given way to a single new one. "I don't know," she said, "why grown-ups can't get along."

You can see that without the conscience, energy, and courage of young people from Ebeneezer Fox to Samantha Smith, American history might be very different. Next, meet a group of young people who are making a difference in their own communities and throughout the world right now.

PART ONE

YOUNG PEOPLE
WHO ARE MAKING
A DIFFERENCE

TAKING A STAND

I FOR ONE AM GRATEFUL FOR THE COURAGE OF YOUTH.
— ELEANOR ROOSEVELT

NETO VILLAREAL
AND
ANDY PERCIFIELD

▲ ■ ●
IN HIS SMALL IDAHO SCHOOL, FOOTBALL MEANT EVERY-
THING TO ERNEST ("NETO") VILLAREAL, SIXTEEN, THE TEAM'S STAR
RUNNING BACK. AND YET WHEN HE HEARD FANS SCREAMING RACIAL
INSULTS AT HIM AND HIS HISPANIC-AMERICAN TEAMMATES, HE WON-
DERED HOW HE COULD KEEP PLAYING FOR FANS WHO FELT THAT WAY. THE
INSULTS ALSO BOTHERED ANDY PERCIFIELD, A WHITE STUDENT LEADER.
WHEN NETO AND ANDY TEAMED UP, EACH USING HIS OWN SPECIAL
POWER, FANS BEGAN TO FEEL HEAT THEY HAD NEVER FELT BEFORE.

When the whistle blew, ending football practice, Jesse
Paz and Ernesto ("Neto") Villareal unsnapped their helmets
and jogged off the field together in silence. Neto could sense
that something was bothering Jesse. Maybe he was worried
about losing his position as first string quarterback.

Just before they reached the locker room, Jesse stopped.
"Aren't you getting tired of white fans yelling at us Hispanic
players?" he asked Neto. "They yell we're no good whenever we mess up. Haven't you heard that at the games?"

"I never really paid attention to it," Neto replied. Something about this made him uncomfortable.

Jesse kept on, his voice rising in anger. "We shouldn't
stand for it. We should quit the team. We have twenty-one
players on the team, and ten of us are Hispanic. Most of the
best players are Hispanic. Without us, there wouldn't even
be a team. If we quit, we could wake up this whole community."

▲ ▲ ● ■
"ANYONE WHO THINKS
WHITES AND HISPANICS
ARE DIFFERENT IS WRONG.
I'M NOT DIFFERENT."
— NETO VILLAREAL
■ ● ■ ■

This was the last thing in the world Neto wanted to hear. For him, football wasn't the problem. Football was the one thing that had made life possible with whites.

Before football, there had been fights with white students almost every day at recess. The whites had kicked them with boots as sharp as spurs. Neto and his Hispanic friends had wrapped little chains around their fists and punched the white kids back.

Until football, there hadn't even been a chance to get to know whites around Marsing, Idaho. Most of the Hispanic families had come to Idaho from Texas or Mexico to pick beets. They lived together in one part of town. White families lived in another. Many Hispanics spoke only Spanish, and most whites spoke only English. They went to different churches.

Every summer since he was seven, Neto had worked from dawn till dusk with his family in the beet fields, chopping up clusters of beets with a metal hoe. Every now and then a white worker would join the Hispanics in the beet fields, but they would usually give up after two or three days. Neto grew up thinking that if more whites knew what it was like to work that hard, they couldn't possibly think they were better than he was.

Now, as a 220-pound tenth-grader, Neto was the starting fullback and middle linebacker on the Marsing High School football team. He loved to lower his shoulder and blast through a thicket of arms and bodies. He was a star player on an exciting team. On Friday nights, hundreds of people from all around the valley piled into trucks, cars, and vans and headed to Marsing Field to watch the Huskies.

Now Jesse Paz was proposing to take away the thing Neto loved most, to turn him into just another big kid at school and maybe even ruin his chance for a college scholarship, all because a few jerks had said things that turned Jesse off. Neto didn't answer for a while. Finally he said, "I've never heard anyone say those things, Jesse," and walked away.

But Jesse's words stayed with Neto. What if it were

true? Could he really perform before people who felt that way about him? Could he represent a school that would let it happen?

"The next game, I decided to see if I could hear what Jesse was hearing," Neto recalls. "In one play, we were running a pass pattern that ended up very near the Marsing cheering section. Our receiver, who was Hispanic, dove for the ball and missed it. Suddenly I could hear voices in our crowd saying, 'Get that stupid Mexican off of there! Put in a white player! G-D those f—— Mexicans!' I looked up. Most of the voices belonged to parents. One was a guy on the school board.

"All game long I kept listening. When a white player would drop a pass, they'd go, 'Nice try.' But they were always negative toward us. Our whole race. I guess I had been blocking it out. Jesse was right. We couldn't just ignore it anymore."

"If You Guys Quit, We'll Lose."

After the game, Neto found Jesse at his locker and said he was ready to act. They called a team meeting. All the players — white and Hispanic — were invited, but not coaches.

The players sat down together on the benches in the locker room. Jesse and Neto repeated the words they had heard and said it hurt too badly for them to play in the next game.

"Yeah, I've heard those things, too," said one player. "Sure it's terrible, but you can't quit! If you guys leave, it will destroy our team."

"Look," Neto said, "if we don't take a stand now, those fans will say those things forever. Even after we graduate, they'll keep putting Hispanic players down. We have a chance to stop it now."

Finally there was no more to say. The question came: "Who votes not to play the next game?" Every player raised his hand.

That night, Neto, Jesse, and another teammate walked into the coach's office and handed him their uniforms and pads. They explained why they were leaving and expected him to understand, but they were disappointed. "The coach said, 'Quitting will just make it worse,'" Neto remembers. "He said the fans would call us losers and quitters instead of respecting us. Nothing could convince him. After a while we just walked out." Now there was no turning back.

"Is There Any Way You Can Help?"

There was no one to talk to when Neto went home that night. His father was no longer living at home, and his mother was away on a trip. Neto made a sandwich, sat down, and looked through the kitchen window at the autumn sky. It wasn't enough just to quit the team, he decided. They had to tell the community why they were quitting, so the fans would at least have a chance to change. But how?

Neto decided to ask Andy Percifield for help. Percifield was the student council president, a tall, red-haired senior who always read the morning announcements over the P.A. system. Neto didn't know him, but people who did said Percifield was smart and fair. Maybe he would know what to do.

Andy Percifield, the student council president who used his power as a school leader to help the striking players.

Neto was waiting by Andy's locker the next morning. "He had tears in his eyes," Andy remembers. "He said that adult fans were swearing at the Mexican players and that it wasn't fair. He was really hurting. He said, 'Is there any way you can help?' I told him I'd try."

When Neto left, Andy walked into the principal's office and repeated Neto's story. He asked for the school's support in dealing with the crowd. "The principal told me he hadn't heard adults say those things," Andy recalls. "He said some of the parents would have to call him and complain before the school administration could get involved. He said Neto had probably heard it out of context anyway." Andy stormed out angrily.

Soon there was even worse news for Neto and Jesse. Most of the players who had voted not to play had suddenly changed their minds. Even the Hispanic players. They could barely look at Neto and Jesse as they explained that they loved football too much to give it up. In the end, only four players — Jesse, Neto, Rigo Delgudillo, and Johnny Garcia — were committed to staying off the field.

The more Neto thought about it, the more determined he became. "I knew we were right," he recalls. "I didn't care what anybody else thought. And I also knew the team couldn't afford to lose me. If the school really wanted me, the fans had to stop saying those things. Only then would I play. Not until."

▲ ▲ ● ■
SOMETIMES TO BE SILENT
IS TO LIE.
— SPANISH PHILOSOPHER
MIGUEL UNAMUNO
■ ■ ● ■ ■

"I COULDN'T BELIEVE I WAS REALLY DOING THIS."

That afternoon, an Hispanic teacher named Baldimar Elizondo, whom everyone called Baldy, suggested that Neto tell the school board about the racist remarks. It was important to say in public why they were quitting, Baldy said, so that the school couldn't ignore it or pretend the protest was about something else.

The board was meeting that night. Baldy offered to pick Neto up and take him. Neto hesitated. He knew he had the courage to blast through tacklers and the toughness to work all day in the beet fields, but this seemed harder. When

Jesse Paz said he'd go, Neto finally agreed.

Baldy picked up Neto first, but when they got to Jesse's, Jesse was nowhere to be found. Now Neto had to choose: did he testify alone or forget it? "All right," Neto finally said, letting out a long breath. "We've gone this far. Let's finish it."

When they entered the board's meeting room, Neto was terrified. They were alone with the ten white men who were the members of the Marsing school board. "I couldn't believe I was really doing this," Neto recalls. "Then I heard Baldy say, 'Neto wants to talk with you about the football team.'

"So I just started. I told them I was quitting and why. I told them word-for-word what I had heard. Only one of them looked like he was really listening. When I was finished, they thanked me for coming, but they didn't say they would do anything about it. I went home thinking, Well, at least I tried. Now they can't say nobody told them."

THE LETTER

Andy Percifield had been busy, too. There were only two days before the next game. He was determined that his school would do the right thing, no matter what the principal said. He had an idea: maybe the students themselves could write a letter against racism that could be read over the microphone in the press box to everyone at the game. It would have to be powerful enough to satisfy the protesting players and shame the racist fans.

Andy was inspired by Neto. Neto was willing to risk his football career, his main source of power and popularity at Marsing High, for something that was right. Andy considered his own power: as council president, he could get out of class more easily than any other student. He could use the office photocopy machine whenever he wanted, and nobody ever asked him what he was reproducing. He read the morning announcements every day, so he could speak to the whole student body. If Neto was willing to risk it all, so was he.

The next morning during study hall, Andy drafted a letter from the students, ran off a hundred copies, and then went to the office microphone to read the morning announcements. "There will be a student council meeting in the chemistry lab at ten," he said. "Attendance is required. Then there will be a meeting of all students in the same room at 10:30. Attendance is encouraged."

At 10:30, students from all grades packed themselves into the lab. Andy stood up and reported what was happening, then read his letter aloud and asked for suggestions to improve it. There were a few. Then he asked for, and got, the students' unanimous approval to have it read at halftime. Next, Andy took the letter to the striking players and asked if it was good enough for them. They studied it carefully. It read:

> *We, the student body of Marsing High School are appalled by the racist behavior of certain people in the audience. Not only does this set a bad example for some younger students, it also reflects very badly on our entire school and community.*
>
> *Although we appreciate the support of our fans for our team, which is composed of students from many ethnic backgrounds, we do not need bigots here.*
>
> *We are asking the authorities to eject from the premises anyone making such rude and racist remarks.*
> *— Marsing High School Student Body*

The four players looked up and grinned. You get this letter read to the crowd, they said, and we'll play. Since the letter wouldn't get read till halftime, Andy said they would have to start the game and trust him. They looked at each other. "You got it," said Neto.

A HOMECOMING LECTURE

Andy had the students and the strikers behind him, but he still needed permission to read the letter. He took it to the principal, hoping for a change of heart. The principal read it, handed it back, and refused permission. They looked at

23

each other. "I kept asking him, 'Well, how are we going to solve this problem?'" Andy recalls. "He didn't have an answer."

Andy was down to his last card: the school superintendent, the most powerful official in the Marsing school district. If he said no, the students would have to act outside school channels. That would be tougher, but not impossible.

Baldy went with Andy to see the superintendent. The superintendent listened carefully to Andy's story and read the letter. "Then he looked up and said he was proud of us," Andy recalls. "He said he would be willing to read the letter himself if we wanted him to. I said no, we wanted to do it ourselves."

On the morning of the homecoming game, while other students were constructing floats and preparing for a parade, Andy Percifield was in the office photocopying one thousand copies of the students' letter. After school, he passed them out to the students who would be working as parking lot attendants at the game and told them to make sure two copies of the students' letter were handed into every car that entered the lot.

At halftime, as homecoming floats circled the field, Allison Gibbons, a member of the student council, entered the press box, stood before the microphone, and asked for everyone's attention. The crowd grew silent as she began to read the letter.

"I was watching the crowd while Allison read it," Andy said. "When she finished, there was silence, and then almost everyone stood up and cheered. All the students stood up. And the football players were all clapping. It was a wonderful feeling to know that we had people behind us."

Since that letter was read, there have been no more racial slurs from the Marsing Husky fans, at least none loud enough for the players to hear. Neto and Andy know that they and Jesse and Rigo and Johnny didn't do away with racial prejudice in their town. Many white parents still won't let their sons and daughters date Hispanics, and the two groups still don't mix much outside school. But they also know that they did what no one before them had done. "At least," says Neto, "we made it known that we wouldn't accept racism in our school or from our fans. We made a difference in the part of our lives that we really could control."

Marsing Huskies Neto Villareal (*number 26*) and Johnny Garcia, two of the Hispanic players who refused to play football for their school until fans stopped yelling racist remarks.

SARAH ROSEN

■▲ ■ ●
One day Sarah Rosen's sixth-grade teacher announced that their school would be reenacting the Constitutional Convention of 1787. But, he said, only boys could take part since only men had participated in the convention. Sarah was furious, but she seemed to be the only one who cared enough to do anything about it. How could one girl change the whole school?

At first it sounded like a great idea to Sarah Rosen and her classmates in Mr. Starczewski's sixth grade class. Students at the Muessel School in South Bend, Indiana, would reenact the Constitutional Convention of 1787, where delegates from twelve of the thirteen new states drew up and signed the U.S. Constitution.

Mr. Star — that's what everyone called their teacher — explained that each of the fourth, fifth, and sixth grade classes would be a state. Students in each class would elect delegates, who would dress up in costumes of the time and pretend to be the original delegates to the convention. Mr. Star said that their class would be South Carolina, and that they would elect four delegates.

Sarah looked around the room, measuring her chances to be elected. There were twenty-one students in her class, ten girls and eleven boys. She was well known and liked, but so were plenty of others. Well, maybe, she thought.

And then Mr. Star dropped the bomb. "Half the class isn't going to like this," he said. "But only boys can be delegates, and only boys will be allowed to vote for delegates."

Sarah felt tears beginning to build as she raised her hand. "Why can't girls be delegates?"

▲ ▲ ● ■ ▬▬▬
"All men are created equal."
— The Declaration of Independence, 1776
▬▬▬ ▬ ● ■ ■

26

Mr. Star explained that the teachers wanted the event to be as close to history as possible. Since there had been no women delegates back then in Philadelphia, he said, there would be no girl delegates now at Muessel School.

Sarah hated discrimination of any kind. She didn't care what had happened two hundred years ago. To her, this was just plain discrimination against girls. Besides, nearly half the boys in the school, and in her class, were black or Asian or Hispanic. Two hundred years ago, they would have been left out, too. The black boys would have been slaves, without the right to vote, and Hispanics and Asians hadn't immigrated to the United States yet. But at Muessel, only girls were going to be left out. What did that say about how her teacher felt about the rights of women?

Sarah wanted to say a million things at once, but she knew she didn't speak well when she was angry. She waited for the bell to ring, then rushed past her friends to her locker and boarded the bus.

"You Have to Do What You Have to Do."

She was already crying by the time she got home. "Sarah, what's wrong?" her mother said. She wiped her tears on her sleeve and told the story. The telling itself seemed to clear her head. And an idea came: she would organize a counterdemonstration of the girls in her class. Let the boys walk around in costumes and pretend to be delegates if they wanted. The girls would take to the halls, chanting and singing in protest. They would represent the women the Constitution forgot back in 1787.

There wasn't much time to lose. It was Friday night, and the mock convention was scheduled for the next Wednesday. Sarah picked up the phone and called the classmates she thought she could count on the most, Jennifer Spinsky and the Wiand sisters, Betsy and Jennifer. They were angry, too. One idea led to another — signs they could make, songs they could sing. They made up chants and slogans.

When Sarah hung up, her mother took the phone and

▲ ▲ ● ■■■■■

"I LONG TO HEAR THAT YOU HAVE DECLARED AN INDEPENDENCY — AND BY THE WAY IN YOUR NEW CODE OF LAWS WHICH I SUPPOSE IT WILL BE NECESSARY FOR YOU TO MAKE I DESIRE YOU WOULD REMEMBER THE LADIES, AND BE MORE GENEROUS AND FAVOURABLE TO THEM THAN YOUR ANCESTORS. DO NOT PUT SUCH UN-LIMITED POWER INTO THE HANDS OF THE HUSBANDS. REMEMBER ALL MEN WOULD BE TY-RANTS IF THEY COULD."
—ABIGAIL ADAMS, IN A LETTER TO HER HUSBAND, JOHN, A DELEGATE TO THE CONTINENTAL CONGRESS, MARCH 31, 1776

■■■■ ● ■ ■

called the principal, Dr. Calvin, to object as a parent to the all-male convention. Sarah listened carefully to her mother's end of the conversation. It sounded as though Dr. Calvin didn't even know about the boys-only rule.

Her mother handed the phone to Sarah. Dr. Calvin said she agreed the rule was wrong. She would gather the teachers before school on Monday morning and give them a choice: either they had to let girls in or, to be accurate to the period, they also had to keep out boys who weren't white. It would be up to each teacher. "Come see me second period on Monday," Dr. Calvin said.

When Sarah got to school on Monday, she went right to Mr. Star. She wanted to know which way he had decided. He seemed amused. Nothing had changed at all, he said.

"But didn't Dr. Calvin tell you?" Sarah asked.

His voice hardened. No changes, and that was final.

When the bell for second hour rang, Sarah went into the principal's office. Dr. Calvin closed the door. "Well?" she said. Sarah reported her conversation with Mr. Star.

Dr. Calvin frowned. Sarah looked at her, trying to decide whether to tell her that she was organizing a protest. It was an important decision. If Dr. Calvin approved, they could use the halls without fear of punishment, no matter what the teachers said. And it would be easier to talk her classmates into it if Sarah could assure them they wouldn't get in trouble with the principal.

But if Dr. Calvin didn't approve, she would be watching for them and she would tell the teachers. There would be no way to surprise them then. And kids would be scared.

Sarah decided to risk it. Dr. Calvin was a woman, and she was black. Probably she had known discrimination in her own life. Even if she said no, Sarah was determined to protest anyway. There were only three days left to organize. She might as well find out what she was up against now.

"Dr. Calvin," Sarah said tentatively, "if Mr. Star isn't going to change his mind, some of us are planning to demonstrate in the halls during the convention."

Sarah thought there might have been a faint smile on

28

the principal's lips. Dr. Calvin shrugged. "Well," she said, "then I guess you have to do what you have to do."

UNEXPECTED HELP

Sarah climbed the ladder to the wooden loft in the back of the classroom and surveyed her classmates. The loft had been built by a group of parents to give the children a quiet place away from their work tables to read and study. Out of Mr. Star's sight, the protesting girls met in the loft each day to make posters.

Of the fifteen girls in the classroom, eight had told Sarah they were solidly behind the protest. A ninth had said she wanted to play in the school band at the convention. That left six. They would probably do whatever Ashley did.

Ashley was a pretty and popular girl who was well aware of her social power. She had groaned like all the other girls when Mr. Star had announced his decision, but she hadn't done anything since. Sarah decided she needed to know where Ashley stood before she went after anyone else.

From the loft, Sarah saw Ashley walk to the drinking fountain in the back of the classroom. Sarah climbed down and asked Ashley if she was planning to demonstrate. No, Ashley said, it was wrong to spoil a day of celebration by doing something disruptive. Sarah tried to keep her temper in check. She couldn't afford to anger Ashley. "I know what you mean," she said thoughtfully. "But how can you celebrate when we're being discriminated against?" A "don't push me" look flickered across Ashley's face. She said she'd think about it and walked away.

Soon Sarah saw Andy Bauer coming toward her. What did *he* want? The boys had elected Andy as a delegate that morning. Maybe he wanted to gloat.

He was grinning. "I quit," he said triumphantly. "I've already written a resignation letter to Mr. Star. I told him I didn't want to be a delegate because it wasn't fair to the girls. Mr. Star just said, 'If that's what you want to do.' Now the other boys say they won't take my place as a delegate."

Sarah was thrilled. This would energize everyone. Now Mr. Star was in a real jam. Where would he get delegates if the boys wouldn't serve and the girls couldn't?

But when a second boy tried to resign, Mr. Star went to a different class and borrowed a boy delegate. And he announced that after Andy, he would allow no other delegates to quit. There was a "that's final" sound to his voice. The other boy delegates quickly returned to studying their South Carolinian characters.

Though she didn't admit it to anyone, even Sarah was a little scared. This was only the second week of school, and Sarah didn't really know Mr. Star. He controlled everything from their grades to how much recess they could have. If he formed an early impression of her as a troublemaker, he could make the rest of the year miserable. Word was already around the school that all the teachers except Mrs. Mills and Mr. Star were letting girls take part. Mrs. Mills was keeping out girls *and* boys of color. That made Mr. Star the only teacher with an anti-girl policy. Sarah wasn't about to back down, and now it was clear Mr. Star wouldn't either. She hoped she wasn't headed for big trouble.

MARCHING FOR EQUAL RIGHTS

Sarah woke on the day of the march excited and nervous. She lay in bed, looking around her room at posters of Martin Luther King, Mohandas Gandhi, and Marilyn Monroe. Her outfit for the day, a green-and-pink blouse and a pink skirt, was hanging neatly on her door. She thought the combination made her look strong and pretty at the same time.

She wondered how many people would protest. Ashley still hadn't said for sure, and neither had Ashley's friends. One thing that might make a difference was that one of the protesters' parents had called a reporter from the local paper. The reporter and a photographer were supposed to show up outside Mr. Star's class at 9:45. Maybe when the undecided girls saw the chance to get in the paper, they would join. Sarah hoped so. She would prefer that every marcher

Sarah Rosen (*in glasses at left*) marches with her classmates against sexism.

be dedicated to women's rights, but she'd let people join for whatever reasons they wanted to.

At 9:45, the delegates left the classroom with Mr. Star. The other students were supposed to wait in the classroom. Instead, the protesting girls — and four boys led by Andy Bauer — went out into the hall with their signs and posters.

The reporter and photographer were waiting for them as they assembled in a two-by-two line. Every girl in the class except one was there, including Ashley, who was holding a big sign. "Women Demand Equality!" it said. "Women Are People!" said another. Sarah grabbed her own sign and placed it squarely in front of her. It read: "We the People." "People" was crossed out and "White Men" put in its place. "Okay," she said. "Let's go!" They began to move forward, singing "We Shall Overcome."

Voices ringing, they tromped down the stairs to where the kids in the lower grades had their classrooms. Some teachers let their children cluster in the doorways to cheer the marchers. But one teacher snapped, "Be quiet!" and slammed the classroom door.

Sarah felt powerful inside; she was acting on her beliefs. In the beginning, Mr. Star had told them, "Half the class isn't going to like this," but he didn't seem to expect that they would actually do something about it.

When the delegates returned to the classrooms, so did the marchers. Word came from the office that three other reporters were waiting to interview Sarah.

Later, when she had time to think, Sarah asked herself what had they accomplished. She didn't believe the protest had changed Mr. Star. He seemed just as set in his ways. He told the reporters that he had left girls out on purpose to cause controversy and teach them a lesson about the fight for the right of women to vote. She didn't believe him for a minute.

But maybe she and the other students had changed. They had taken a stand for something they believed in. They had shown that they wouldn't accept being discriminated against. A lot of younger kids had seen them and were asking the protesters questions about why they had done it. Surely it would be harder for their school to plan something unfair again.

Most important of all to Sarah, they had probably raised consciousness about women's rights in their school. By her action, she had said that she was as good as anyone else and deserved a chance to share in whatever the school had to offer. As Dr. Calvin had put it, she did what she had to do.

▲ ▲ ● ▬▬▬

"OUR LESSON ON THE CONSTITUTION TAUGHT ME SOMETHING. IT TAUGHT ME FIRSTHAND THAT IF YOU WANT SOMETHING CHANGED, YOU HAVE TO DO IT."
— SARAH ROSEN

▬▬▬ ● ■ ■

NORVELL SMITH

■ ■ ● **O**NE DAY WHEN SHE WAS TWELVE, **N**ORVELL **S**MITH FOUND HERSELF SURROUNDED BY GANG MEMBERS WHO PRESSURED HER TO JOIN THEIR GANG. **T**O SAY YES MEANT EXCITEMENT AND MONEY. **I**T ALSO MEANT A LIFE OF CRIME AND POSSIBLY AN EARLY DEATH. **B**UT TO SAY NO SEEMED EVEN MORE DANGEROUS.

As the jangling sound of the last bell echoed through the halls of John Hope School, Norvell Smith clutched her books and fought through the crowd toward her locker. She stuffed some papers inside, grabbed her jacket, and ran for the door. But when she burst outside, she could see her bus disappearing.

Already it was getting dark. Norvell knew her mother would worry, and with good reason. Her school, in the South Side of Chicago, was part of a virtual war zone. Gang members and drug pushers struggled to control the streets around it.

One side of the boulevard in front of Hope School belonged to the Folks. They wore blue and black. The other side belonged to the Brothers. They wore red and black, with their baseball cap bills pushed to the left. Every year since first grade, at least one kid in her grade school had been shot in gang crossfire.

Norvell didn't like walking home alone, but there was no alternative. She decided to try a shortcut through Sherman Park. She didn't know the park well, but there was still a little daylight.

She was about halfway through the park when she saw five high-school girls watching her. They were all wearing blue and black. She began to pray that they wouldn't mess with her.

She kept her head down as she walked rapidly toward the bridge that connected Sherman Park with her neighborhood. One of the girls moved forward to block her way. The others followed. The leader was tall, hard-faced, and razor thin. She placed a long, tapered red fingernail on Norvell's chest.

"What's up?" she said.

"Nothin'."

"We've been watchin' you."

"Me? Why?" Norvell's throat was dry. She struggled to keep her voice steady.

"You want to be down with us?" the leader said.

"No," Norvell said, "I don't." She could hardly believe the words had come out of her mouth. Was she crazy?

The leader seemed surprised. "Why not?" she said.

Norvell hesitated. Then the flat truth came out. "Because I don't want to disappoint my mama."

They began to chuckle. The leader stooped down and put her face in Norvell's.

"F—— your mama," she said. "She don't have nothin' to do with this."

Norvell felt a surge of anger.

"My mama has everything to do with this," she said firmly, looking straight back. "She raised seven kids without a problem. I'm not going to be the first."

No one spoke. There was only a trace of pale light in the sky to the west. The leader pointed to her jacket.

"You see these colors?" she said proudly. "When you're in the Folks, all the little kids will look up to you. You'll have friends. If you ever get in trouble, we'll stick up for you."

Yeah, Norvell was thinking, but what if I don't want trouble?

Norvell decided to make her move. She would try to make it to the bridge. If she could get across, she might be able to lose them in her neighborhood. She thought about her first steps, looked straight at the leader, and spoke in the biggest voice she could find. "No," she said. "It's my decision. I don't want to be in your gang."

She began to walk forward. No one stopped her. She quickened her steps as the dark form of the bridge came into view. She didn't look back, but she heard only her own footsteps on the path. When she got to the bridge, she began to sprint. She didn't stop until she was through her front door and into her room. She fell belly down on her bed, gasping.

Her mother rushed in through the open bedroom door. "She said, 'What's wrong with you? What's wrong with you?'" Norvell recalls. "I said, 'Mom, please, just let me alone for a while.' When she left, I got up and looked in the mirror. I said, 'You really said those things, didn't you? Girl, I can't *believe* you.'"

"WHY ME?"

Two years later, when Norvell was in eighth grade, her teacher announced that a police organization was sponsoring a speech contest. Every student at John Hope School would have to write a speech about guns, drugs, gangs, or interpersonal violence. The winner would get to read his or her speech to the entire school and receive a plaque.

Norvell thought about it. She'd love to tell the world about those girls in Sherman Park. About how hard it had been to say no. But only a fool would write a speech against gangs. Too many of the kids in her school were in them. She wasn't that dumb.

Some of her friends made big money in gangs. Adults who sold crack paid young gang members to help them fight for control of the streets. Unfortunately, one of the hottest corners was right in front of Norvell's house. Every night when Norvell got off the bus at Seventy-ninth and Pelina, she walked past the drug dealers. People in cars would cruise up to them and roll down the windows an inch or two, their motors still idling. After a few words the driver would push some cash out to the dealer. The dealer would pull crack vials out of a shopping bag under his jacket, pass them through the window, and the car would pull away.

Sometimes the older dealers even paid the kids on her block to sell drugs for them, so the adults wouldn't get arrested and sent to jail. Norvell knew kids who walked around with hundreds of dollars in cash stuffed in the pockets of their jackets and jeans.

Norvell was never tempted to use drugs, but she prayed every night for the strength to keep from selling them. She knew how badly her family needed money. Her mother barely made enough as a cook in a downtown restaurant to pay for her cab fare home each night. Sometimes, when Norvell and her brother watched TV programs about kids in the suburbs with nice houses in safe neighborhoods without gangs, she was jealous. Those kids probably didn't even know what a gunshot sounded like. They wouldn't know a crack vial if they saw one. Sometimes when she watched those shows, she couldn't help herself from wondering, "Why me? Why do I have to live here?"

GRASSHOPPER

Norvell opened her English notebook and started to write a speech about something that seemed relatively safe: saying no to drugs.

But for some reason the picture of those girls in the park kept coming back to her. And there was another picture, too. It was the face of her friend Charles Brown, Grasshopper, as she called him.

One afternoon just the week before, Charles and his cousin, a member of the Folks, had walked out of school and crossed the Boulevard. Soon they'd been joined by two boys in baseball caps, wearing black and red, who had begun to taunt Charles's cousin. There was shouting — and a shot. The bullet struck a brick building, bounced off, and went straight into Charles's spine. Grasshopper was dead in an instant. When Norvell found out, it felt like the bullet had hit her, too. Grasshopper had been one boy in eighth grade she could really talk to. Now he was dead.

Norvell crumpled up the beginning of her "just say no to drugs" speech. Why not say what really needed to be said? Why not say how stupid gangs were. How unfair. What did she really have to lose when she lived in a place where you could be killed by a stray bullet just crossing the street? She was going to make her life count for something. Shaking her head to clear it, Norvell tore off a fresh sheet of paper and began to write.

"Go Up There and Do What You Have to Do."

The school auditorium was filled on the afternoon Norvell was to speak. First her teacher had told her she had been chosen one of the final twenty, then one of the top three, and then the winner. Now she would stand on stage and give her speech to all 330 students in her school.

As she listened to a teacher introduce her, all Norvell could think about were the dozens of gang members seated in the audience. She was about to tell them they had all made stupid decisions. She wondered if she would make it out of the auditorium alive.

"I was terrified," Norvell recalls. "I whispered to Mrs. Cooney, my teacher, before I spoke, 'Please drive me home if this doesn't work out.' She said, 'Don't worry, I will. Just go up there and do what you have to do.' "

When she heard her name, Norvell stepped to the microphone and looked out at her schoolmates. All she could see were colors: blue and black, red and black. The gang members were slouched in their seats, smirking, looking up at her. For a moment, she didn't know if she could do it. And then, just as she had somehow found her strong voice in Sherman Park, she heard it again, saying, "I'm here today to talk about gangs."

She spoke slowly and steadily, pausing from time to time to let people think about her words. "I'm sick and tired," she said, "of these people coming into our neighborhoods and putting ideas into our little brothers' and sisters' minds that gangs are cool." Whenever she paused there was total silence. She couldn't believe it — they were actually listening.

By the time she reached the end, her fear was gone. She finished by telling them the truth as plainly as she knew how: "I say the only thing that you can get out of being in a gang is a hole in your head or six feet under — take your choice."

With that, she picked up her speech and started to sit down. They were all standing to applaud her — even the gang members! People rushed forward to congratulate her. Mrs. Cooney, eyes shining, asked Norvell if she wanted a ride home. "No," Norvell said, looking around and smiling in disbelief. "I think I'll take the bus."

"YOU CAN'T TELL ME WHAT TO DO!"

Norvell entered her speech in a citywide competition and won again. A Chicago newspaper wrote a story about her. Soon she felt that her classmates seemed to resent the attention she was getting. She found terrible things written about her on the rest room walls. One day there was an unsigned note in her locker saying, "You better shut up." A rumor circulated at school that someone was out to beat her up. For weeks, security guards at her school walked her out to her bus at night.

But there was a bright side, too. Teachers from around the city began to call her to see if she could talk to their young students. The police department offered other chances to speak.

She decided to try speaking to a classroom of fifth-graders. Right away she discovered how hard it was to reach some kids. "I was telling them I used to think, 'Well, maybe I *should* join a gang because that way I would never get beat up,' " Norvell recalls. "I said that I found out that when the going gets tough, sometimes gang members desert you."

Suddenly a boy stood up, eyes blazing, and pointed straight at her. "You can't tell me what to do," he said defiantly. "This is *my* life."

Norvell was startled. This boy was furious. And he was

right. It *was* his life. The children looked at Norvell, wondering how she would answer him. She struggled to find the words she wanted. "You're right," she said finally. "If you want to die in a gang, it's your choice."

After her speech, she asked the boy if they could talk. He walked away, cursing her. Later, his teacher told Norvell the boy had two brothers in gangs. They were his heroes.

Norvell felt like a failure. She got home, sank into a chair, and told her mother she was ready to quit speaking. "I remember my momma said, 'Girl, don't worry about it. That was your first time. You'll do better.'"

The next time, she tried something different. "I started talking to the boys about their mothers," she says. "That's the one thing that'll make 'em stop and think. They'll be thinking, 'My mother loves me. And if I messed up, she would kill me.' It taught me something about speaking: you can say the same thing several ways, depending on who you're talking to."

"HERE, I CAN COUNT."

Now Norvell is sixteen and is busily recruiting a team of young people to speak out against gangs. She is looking for kids ranging from grade-schoolers to high-schoolers to speak to kids their own age. She plans to ask companies to sponsor

Norvell Smith (*center*) with Aisha Cecil (*left*) and Melba Timmons (*right*), who speak out against gangs with her in Chicago.

her speakers and dreams of speaking in other cities.

Not long ago, Norvell happened to meet one of the gang members who had tried to recruit her in Sherman Park. Now she is a young single mother, living at home with no job and no plans. Norvell started to tell her about a night school program at her high school, but the girl looked away. After an awkward silence, Norvell started to walk on. The girl called her name. "Norvell," she said. "I'm glad that you didn't say yes to us that day. I know about you. You're doing good. Keep going."

The threats still come Norvell's way. "Each time before I speak, I pray that Jesus will protect me. So far, I'm still here." Scary as it is, speaking to the children of Chicago's violent South Side has helped her answer her old question. "Maybe the reason I'm growing up here," she says, "and not out in the suburbs, is that here I have a chance to make a difference. Here, I can count."

JOHN DeMARCO

■ ▪ ● **ONE DAY WHEN HE WAS THIRTEEN, JOHN DEMARCO SAW A NEIGHBOR PAINTING RACIST SLOGANS ON A HOUSE TO SCARE A BLACK FAMILY FROM MOVING INTO HIS PHILADELPHIA NEIGHBORHOOD. SOON A COP CAME AROUND ASKING WHO DID IT. JOHN THOUGHT ABOUT WHETHER TO TELL. NOT TO SAY WOULD BE WRONG. BUT TO TELL MIGHT ANGER HIS NEIGHBORS AND PLACE HIS FAMILY IN DANGER. WHAT SHOULD HE DO?**

John DeMarco stepped out onto the porch of his mother's small red-brick house on the North Side of Philadelphia, raised his hand above his eyes, and squinted into the glare of a hot July day. Was that shouting he heard? Maybe there was a fight. John looked down Sellers Street to see what was happening. A group of neighbors were clustered around a house across the street and down the block. They were laughing and yelling and pumping their fists in the air. Curious, John walked across the street, stood on his tiptoes, and looked over the backs of two laughing neighbors. Richard Keller, whose sister lived on the block, was spraying something on the front of the building with a can of bright blue paint. John leaned forward to read the words: "We Don't Want No Niggers. KKK." The others were cheering Richard on. "That's right! That'll show them!"

John went back home and watched from his steps. It looked like something from a film he had seen at school about Martin Luther King. But this was Sellers Street, not Mississippi. How could this be happening here, on his block?

Then he remembered that earlier, he had seen a tall, nicely dressed black woman and four children step out of a car driven by a real estate agent in front of that same house.

41

It had been for sale for a long time. If they bought the house, they would be the first black people on the block. Apparently, this bright blue message was meant to scare them away.

Someone threw a beer bottle, and more and more people came rushing to the scene, as if the house were a magnet. A neighbor ran out of his house with a white sheet nailed to a stick. They placed it on the ground and sprayed "KKK" on it and started waving it around like a flag, cheering.

John couldn't believe what he was seeing. He wondered how anyone could feel that way. How could you hate someone you didn't even know? Most of his schoolmates were black. Most he liked; some he didn't. But he chose his friends according to whether they were funny or friendly or whether they liked the same things he did, not what they looked like. John went back inside and closed the door, the noise in the street still loud behind him. He had seen enough.

"I'M PROUD OF YOU."

When the doorbell rang the next afternoon, John was in the living room. He stood still, listening, as his mother opened the door. It was a cop. He was asking if Mrs. DeMarco knew who wrote the message in blue spray paint on the house across the street. Of course she knew, John was thinking. By now everybody knew. That was all the neighbors had been talking about.

But his mom hadn't actually seen it happen. He had. John stepped to his mother's side. "I saw it," he interrupted. "It was Richard Keller." The officer looked up, surprised. He had been walking up and down the block all morning, and this stocky blond kid was the first to give a name. The cop scribbled Keller's name in his pad and asked John to describe everything he had seen. Then he thanked John, snapped his pad shut, and walked down the street. When she closed the door behind the cop, Peg DeMarco turned to her son and smiled. "I'm proud of you," she said.

42

A few days later the cop was back again. This time to ask John to go to court and testify against Keller. Why not? he thought. It was the right thing to do.

But John didn't know that he was the only person on his block to name Keller. He found out one afternoon a few days before the court hearing when he was carrying groceries home from the store and a piece of paper nailed to a telephone pole caught his eye. There, looking back at him, was his own face. It was a newspaper photograph. And on it, someone had scrawled the word *rat*.

His heart raced as he stared at the photo. What was his picture doing in the paper? Were people after him?

He quickened his steps toward home. A voice called from across the street, "Hey, DeMarco, why'd you rat on Kathy's brother?" John said nothing and kept on walking, his body stiff with tension.

When he got home, John ran inside to look for the paper. Sure enough, there was the story about the kid who had agreed to testify against the racist spray painter on Sellers Street. The story said he was the only neighbor who had identified thirty-four-year-old Richard Keller.

Suddenly this was no longer a simple question of right and wrong. Now his own safety was on the line. Maybe his life. Keller's sister and mother lived on the block, and many of his friends. Should he testify?

John prided himself on being tough. He was a promising middleweight boxer. His trainer at Reddish Gym had told him that he had the talent to be a champion. But now he was scared.

One night not long before the trial, John found his mother in the kitchen, finishing up the dishes. She was the strongest person he knew. Nothing seemed to get her down, not the nosy neighbors, not the trouble he gave her sometimes, not their lack of money.

John sat down at the table. She waited for the words to come. "Ma," he said finally, "what if they kill us?" There was not a trace of worry in her expression as she turned to look at him. "John," she said, "If we die, we die. It's in the hands of God. But I know this. It's better to die for something you believe in than to die for nothing."

"RICH DID IT."

On a windy day in early November, John DeMarco, wearing the navy blue suit he usually wore to Mass, climbed into the back seat of a police car and rode off with his mother toward downtown Philadelphia. When they arrived at City Hall, they were joined by Amzie Denson, the black woman who had wanted to buy the house across the street, and her daughters. Mrs. Denson shook John's hand and thanked him for his courage. She said they had seen the spray paint and decided not to buy the house. Now they were settled in a different neighborhood. They walked in silence up the marble steps and into the building.

John had never been in court before. Lawyers in business suits mingled with cops in the halls outside the courtroom doors. He noticed that some people were wearing handcuffs. He sat with his mother on a bench outside the courtroom door until the case was called, trying to remember what Mimi Rose, the assistant DA had told him: "Stick to your story, keep it simple, take your time, and don't look at Keller until you have to point him out." He was scared.

The judge banged her gavel for the hearing to begin and Ms. Rose called John to the witness stand. He raised his right hand, swore to tell the truth, and looked out at the people in the courtroom. He knew most of them. On one side, he saw his mother and the Densons. On the other were Richard Keller's friends and relatives. He could see Keller, too, but tried not to look at him.

Ms. Rose got right to the point. "Please point to the man who wrote the 'KKK' on the wall," she said. John pointed to Keller, now looking directly into his eyes. He said simply, "Rich did it."

When Ms. Rose was finished, it was Keller's attorney's turn. John braced for the worst, but it was over in a moment. She asked only that John identify the spray painter again.

Once again, he pointed to Keller. With that, John stepped down from the bench and sat beside his mother. She pressed his hand. Others testified, and then the attorneys gave their closing arguments. "Your honor, my client is needed in the home," said Keller's attorney. "Your client should have thought about that when he was writing those obscenities," replied the judge sharply. And then she gave her verdict: guilty of racial intimidation. One year in jail and a $2,500 fine. Bond was set at $100,000.

It was the toughest possible sentence. A cop snapped handcuffs on Keller and led him out of the courtroom. Keller's family seemed in shock. John tried not to think about their pain as he stepped out into the cold air and reporters and photographers surrounded him on the courthouse steps. They were eager to introduce readers to Philadelphia's newest hero, the boy who had taken a stand and sent a racist to jail. John began to feel more than a little nervous. This might not play too well back on the block.

John DeMarco and Amzie Denson on the courthouse steps just after John's testimony. Hours later, when John got back to his neighborhood, his real troubles began.

45

"THAT'S FOR YOU, JOHN DEMARCO."

The next day, John DeMarco's picture was on the front page of Philadelphia's newspapers. Later that week, news teams from local TV stations set up their cameras by his mother's rosebushes. John's neighbors watched from behind curtains and blinds. Every article, every TV show, every scrap of attention seemed to make some of them hate him more. To them, John DeMarco was no hero. He was a big-mouthed kid who had broken a code of silence. He was getting famous by making them look like scum.

In the next few days, Richard Keller and John DeMarco seemed to trade places. Keller was set free until his case could be appealed (he never did serve time in jail but was ordered to provide community service instead), and Sellers Street became a terrifying sort of prison for John and his family.

After the reporters disappeared, most of John's neighbors turned against him. Bottles were smashed against the DeMarcos' house in the night. Garbage was strewn all over their porch. The phone rang with death threats, and there were hate letters in the mail.

John learned for himself how it feels to be discriminated against. When he walked down the street, most people turned away. Some swore at him. Others spat. Some called him "Rat." At the grocery store, his neighbors would say, "What are you buying, DeMarco, cheese?"

As the threats mounted, police accompanied John to school. School was upsetting in different ways. There the principal was always praising him — which just made things worse. Some black kids he didn't even know treated him as if he had done them a personal favor, while school-mates from his own neighborhood ignored or taunted him. He felt exhausted and sad. He didn't want to be a hero or a rat. He just wanted to be left alone.

It took two years for things to calm down. During that time, John went to live with his aunt. When he finally returned home, most neighbors seemed glad to see him. There had been some changes in the neighborhood while he was gone. Now the DeMarcos had several black and Hispanic neighbors. "I know those people couldn't have moved in if John hadn't done what he did," said Peg DeMarco.

John recently graduated from high school. Sometimes he still thinks about the six words, "I saw it" and "Rich did it," that took away his freedom and happiness a few years ago. But he knows the words gave him something, too. They let him know something about himself that many people never learn in a whole lifetime. He knows that when he was tested, he had the courage to do what was right.

He doesn't think of himself as a hero. "What happened to me was tough, sure," he says. "But what happened to the Denson family was even tougher. They couldn't even move into the house they wanted. All of this changed me. If someone told a racial joke in front of me before, I used to just pretend I didn't hear it, but now I'll step in. And I'll tell you one other thing: if the same thing happened outside my house again today, I'd do it all over again."

REACHING
OUT
TO
OTHERS

**ANYBODY CAN BE GREAT,
BECAUSE ANYBODY CAN SERVE.**

— DR. MARTIN LUTHER KING, JR

**TO HAVE PEACE IN THE WORLD, I THINK
YOU HAVE TO LOOK FIRST AT YOURSELF,
THEN AT YOUR FAMILY, THEN AT YOUR
COMMUNITY AND ON OUT. TO MAKE A
DIFFERENCE IN THE WORLD, YOU FIRST
HAVE TO MAKE A DIFFERENCE WITH
YOURSELF.**

— CAITLIN CHESTNUT, FOURTEEN, PEACE ACTIVIST

JUSTIN LEBO

■▲ ■ ● SINCE HE WAS TEN, JUSTIN LEBO, FOURTEEN, OF
PATERSON, NEW JERSEY, HAS BEEN BUILDING BICYCLES OUT OF USED
PARTS HE FINDS FROM OLD JUNKERS. WHEN HE FINISHES, HE GIVES
THEM AWAY TO KIDS WHO ARE HOMELESS OR SICK. HE PLOWS MOST
OF HIS ALLOWANCE INTO THE PROJECT AND OFTEN WORKS ON NIGHTS
AND WEEKENDS. WHY DOES HE DO IT? THE ANSWER IS SURPRISING.
"IN PART," HE SAYS, "I DO IT FOR MYSELF."

Something about the battered old bicycle at the garage
sale caught ten-year-old Justin Lebo's eye. What a wreck! It
was like looking at a few big bones in the dust and trying to
figure out what kind of dinosaur they had once belonged to.

It was a BMX bike with a twenty-inch frame. Its original
color was buried beneath five or six coats of gunky paint.
Now it showed up as sort of a rusted red. Everything — the
grips, the pedals, the brakes, the seat, the spokes — were
bent or broken, twisted and rusted. Justin stood back as if
he were inspecting a painting for sale at an auction. Then
he made his final judgment: perfect.

Justin talked the owner down to $6.50 and asked his
mother, Diane, to help him load the bike into the back of
their car.

When he got it home, he wheeled the junker into the
garage and showed it proudly to his father. "Will you help
me fix it up?" he asked. Justin's hobby was bike racing, a
passion the two of them shared. Their garage barely had
room for the car anymore. It was more like a bike shop.
Tires and frames hung from hooks on the ceiling, and bike
wrenches dangled from the walls.

After every race, Justin and his father would adjust the
brakes and realign the wheels of his two racing bikes. This

was a lot of work, since Justin raced flat out, challenging every gear and part to perform to its fullest. He had learned to handle almost every repair his father could and maybe even a few things he couldn't. When Justin got really stuck, he went to see Mel, the owner of the best bike shop in town. Mel let him hang out and watch, and he even grunted a few syllables of advice from between the spokes of a wheel now and then.

Now Justin and his father cleared out a work space in the garage and put the old junker up on a rack. They poured alcohol on the frame and rubbed until the old paint began to yield, layer by layer. They replaced the broken pedal, tightened down a new seat, and restored the grips. In about a week, it looked brand new.

Justin wheeled it out of the garage, leapt aboard, and started off around the block. He stood up and mashed down on the pedals, straining for speed. It was a good, steady ride, but not much of a thrill compared to his racers.

Soon he forgot about the bike. But the very next week, he bought another junker at a yard sale and fixed it up, too. After a while it bothered him that he wasn't really using either bike. Then he realized that what he loved about the old bikes wasn't riding them: it was the challenge of making something new and useful out of something old and broken.

Justin wondered what he should do with them. They were just taking up space in the garage. He remembered that when he was younger, he used to live near a large brick building called the Kilbarchan Home for Boys. It was a place for boys whose parents couldn't care for them for one reason or another.

He found "Kilbarchan" in the phone book and called the director, who said the boys would be thrilled to get two bicycles. The next day when Justin and his mother unloaded the bikes at the home, two boys raced out to greet them. They leapt aboard the bikes and started tooling around the semicircular driveway, doing wheelies and pirouettes, laughing and shouting.

Justin Lebo, who has built hundreds of bikes and given them away to kids who are orphaned, ill, or homeless.

The Lebos watched them for a while, then started to climb into their car to go home. The boys cried after them, "Wait a minute! You forgot your bikes!" Justin explained that the bikes were for them to keep. "They were so happy," Justin remembers. "It was like they couldn't believe it. It made me feel good just to see them happy."

On the way home, Justin was silent. His mother assumed he was lost in a feeling of satisfaction. But he was thinking about what would happen once those bikes got wheeled inside and everyone saw them. How would all those kids decide who got the bikes? Two bikes could cause more trouble than they would solve. Actually, they hadn't been that hard to build. It was fun. Maybe he could do more. . . .

"Mom," Justin said as they turned onto their street, "I've got an idea. I'm going to make a bike for every boy at Kilbarchan for Christmas." Diane Lebo looked at Justin out of the corner of her eye. She had rarely seen him so determined.

▲ ▲ ● ▬▬▬▬
"IT IS BY SPENDING ONE'S SELF THAT ONE BECOMES RICH."
— SARAH BERNHARDT
▬▬▬▬ ● ■ ■

When they got home, Justin called Kilbarchan to find out how many boys lived there. There were twenty-one. It was already June. He had six months to make nineteen bikes. That was almost a bike a week. Justin called the home back to tell them of his plan. "I could tell they didn't think I could do it," Justin remembers. "I knew I could."

"IT JUST SNOWBALLED."

Justin knew his best chance was to build bikes almost the way GM or Ford builds cars: in an assembly line. He would start with frames from three-speed, twenty-four-inch BMX bicycles. They were common bikes, and all the parts were interchangeable. If he could find enough decent frames, he could take parts off broken bikes and fasten them onto the good frames. He figured it would take three or four junkers to produce enough parts to make one good bike. That meant sixty to eighty bikes. Where would he get them?

Garage sales seemed to be the only hope. It was June, and there would be garage sales all summer long. But even if he could find that many bikes, how could he ever pay for them? That was hundreds of dollars.

He went to his parents with a proposal. "When Justin was younger, say five or six," says his mother, "he used to give some of his allowance away to help others in need. His father and I would donate a dollar for every dollar Justin donated. So he asked us if it could be like the old days, if we'd match every dollar he put into buying old bikes. We said yes."

Justin and his mother spent most of June and July hunting for cheap bikes at garage sales and thrift shops. They would haul the bikes home, and Justin would start stripping them down in the yard.

But by the beginning of August, he had managed to make only ten bikes. Summer vacation was almost over, and school and homework would soon cut into his time. Garage sales would dry up when it got colder, and Justin was out of money. Still, he was determined to find a way.

At the end of August, Justin got a break. A neighbor wrote a letter to the local newspaper describing Justin's project, and an editor thought it would make a good story. One day a reporter entered the Lebo garage. Stepping gingerly through the tires and frames that covered the floor, she found a boy with cut fingers and dirty nails, banging a seat onto a frame. His clothes were covered with grease. In her admiring article about a boy who was devoting his summer to help kids he didn't even know, she said Justin needed bikes and money, and she printed his home phone number.

Overnight, everything changed. "There must have been a hundred calls," Justin says. "People would call me up and ask me to come over and pick up their old bike. Or I'd be working in the garage, and a station wagon would pull up. The driver would leave a couple of bikes by the curb. It just snowballed."

By the start of school, the garage was overflowing with BMX frames. Pyramids of pedals and seats rose in the corners. Soon bike parts filled a toolshed in the backyard and then spilled out into the small yard itself, wearing away the lawn.

Justin Lebo with some of the bikes he's built.

More and more writers and television and radio reporters called for interviews. Each time he told his story, Justin asked for bikes and money. "The first few interviews were fun," Justin says, "but it reached a point where I really didn't like doing them. The publicity was necessary, though. I had to keep doing interviews to get the donations I needed."

By the time school opened, he was working on ten bikes at a time. There were so many calls now that he was beginning to refuse offers that weren't the exact bikes he needed.

As checks came pouring in, Justin's money problems disappeared. He set up a bank account and began to make bulk orders of common parts from Mel's bike shop. Mel seemed delighted to see him. Sometimes, if Justin brought a bike by the shop, Mel would help him fix it. When Justin tried to talk him into a lower price for big orders, Mel smiled and gave in. He respected another good businessman. They became friends.

"Why Do You Do It?"

The week before Christmas Justin delivered the last of the twenty-one bikes to Kilbarchan. Once again, the boys poured out of the home and leapt aboard the bikes, tearing around the snow.

▲ ▲ ● ▬▬▬▬

"I DON'T THINK YOU CAN
EVER REALLY DO ANY-
THING TO HELP ANY-
BODY ELSE IF IT DOESN'T
MAKE YOU HAPPY."
— JUSTIN LEBO

▬▬▬▬ ● ■ ■

And once again, their joy inspired Justin. They reminded him how important bikes were to him. Wheels meant freedom. He thought how much more the freedom to ride must mean to boys like these who had so little freedom in their lives. He decided to keep on building.

"First I made eleven bikes for the children in a foster home my mother told me about. Then I made bikes for all the women in a battered women's shelter. Then I made ten little bikes and tricycles for the kids in a home for children with AIDS. Then I made twenty-three bikes for the Paterson Housing Coalition."

In the four years since he started, Justin Lebo has made between 150 and 200 bikes and given them all away. He has been careful to leave time for his homework, his friends, his coin collection, his new interest in marine biology, and of course his own bikes.

Reporters and interviewers have asked Justin Lebo the same question over and over: "Why do you do it?" The question seems to make him uncomfortable. It's as if they want him to say what a great person he is. Their stories always make him seem like a saint, which he knows he isn't. "Sure it's nice of me to make the bikes," he says, "because I don't have to. But I want to. In part, I do it for myself. I don't think you can ever really do anything to help anybody else if it doesn't make you happy.

"Once I overheard a kid who got one of my bikes say, 'A bike is like a book; it opens up a whole new world.' That's how I feel, too. It made me happy to know that kid felt that way. That's why I do it."

DWAINA BROOKS

▲ ■ ● **ON FRIDAY NIGHTS, DWAINA BROOKS, ELEVEN, AND AS MANY AS TWENTY-SIX OF HER FRIENDS AND RELATIVES TURN HER MOTHER'S KITCHEN INTO A MEAL FACTORY FOR THE HOMELESS OF DALLAS. WITH THE RADIO SET TO 100.3 — THE RAP STATION — AND WITH MAYONNAISE UP TO THEIR ELBOWS, THEY HAVE PRODUCED AS MANY AS THREE HUNDRED MEALS IN A NIGHT.**

Each morning on her way to school, Dwaina Brooks saw the line of men and women outside a homeless shelter and soup kitchen in Dallas. Many looked cold and sleepy. Sometimes one man stood in the street carrying a sign that said, "I Will Work for Food to Feed My Children." No one ever stopped to talk to him. How could they just pass him by?

At school, her fourth-grade class was doing a unit on homelessness. Once a week, students telephoned a shelter and talked with someone who was staying there. Dwaina would ask the person on the other end of the phone, "How'd you wind up on the streets?" "Do you want to be there?" "What did you do before?" She listened carefully. Most people's lives had been going along okay, and then something bad had happened. They got fired. The family broke up. They couldn't make a rent payment.

Always she asked, "What do you need?" The answer was always "a home," or "a job." It never seemed as though she could do much more than keep sending her lunch money to the shelter. Then one afternoon, Dwaina talked with a young man who had been without a home for a long time.

"What do you need?" she asked him.

"I need a job and a permanent home," he replied.

"Well, I can't give you that," she answered impatiently. "I don't have a job either. Don't you need anything else?"

Dwaina Brooks, who organized her family and friends to feed homeless people in Dallas.

"Yeah. I would love a really good meal again."

"Well, now," said Dwaina, brightening. "I *can* cook."

WHY NOT?

Dwaina tore into the house that night after school and found her mother, Gail. As usual, she was in the kitchen. "Mama," she said. "I need you to help me fix some stuff to take down to that shelter we call at school. Let's make up as much as we can. Sandwiches and chicken. Let's get everyone to do it. C'mon."

Gail Brooks looked at her daughter. All of her children were generous, but Dwaina had always been a little different. Even when she was a baby, Dwaina couldn't stand to see anyone hurt or left out. If she only took one doll to bed with her, pretty soon she would start wondering if all the others felt bad. The next morning, there would be a bed full of dolls and Dwaina on the floor.

Make food for the homeless? Well, why not? They decided to prepare meals on Friday night. They spent the next three days shopping and preparing. Counting Dwaina's lunch money, which she decided to donate to the cause, they figured they had about sixty dollars to spend. Their challenge was how to make that stretch into as many meals as possible.

Coupons helped cut the prices for sandwich wrapping, cookies, and mayonnaise. Dwaina's uncle got them discount lunch meats from the store where he used to work. Thursday night was bargain night at the bakery in nearby Lancaster. They drove away with six big loaves of day-old bread for $1.78. "Mama, do you think anyone at the shelter will really eat day-old bread?" Dwaina asked. "We eat it," Gail replied. "If it don't kill us, it won't kill them."

The baker gave them twenty free boxes, too, when he heard how they would be used. Dwaina's aunts and uncles brought over huge sacks of chips and big bottles of salad dressing.

When Dwaina got home from school on Friday, the stage was set. Her mother's table was covered with a plastic cloth. The plastic gloves from the dime store were laid out. Mountains of ham, turkey, and cheese were at one end. Two rows of bread went from one end of the table to the other. They looked like piano keys. A huge jar of mayonnaise was open and ready.

Dwaina's sisters, Stephanie, sixteen, and Crystal, nine, already had aprons tied around their waists. Dwaina turned on the radio, and they all formed an assembly line and dug in. Gail threw chicken into three skillets and got them all going at once. Dwaina slapped meat on open slices of bread and covered them with mayo. Crystal wrapped sandwiches and stuffed sacks. Dwaina looked on proudly as the corner of the kitchen began to fill up with sacks. It looked like a lot of meals.

It was after ten when the last sack was stuffed. The kitchen looked like a tornado had ripped through it. They placed 105 carefully wrapped meals in the bakery boxes, loaded them in the Oldsmobile, and headed downtown.

When they got to the shelter, two men came out to the street and helped carry in the boxes. Dwaina set down her first box and looked around the shelter. It was a big, open room with beds along the walls. It was dark, but some men were up front in a lighted area drinking coffee. She wondered if the man who had said he wanted a good meal was still living there. If he was, she thought with pride, he sure enough would have a treat tomorrow.

"WHO'LL BE THERE?"

After that, nearly every Friday night for a year, Dwaina and her mother and whatever sisters were around made food for shelters in Dallas. At first they took the food to the shelters themselves, but then their church volunteered to make the deliveries for them.

Always, Dwaina wanted to make more meals. That shelter had hundreds of people; she and her mom alone probably weren't feeding half of them. One Friday evening, she had an idea: she knew where she could get some extra help, and lots of it, too.

The following Monday, she asked her fifth-grade teacher, Mr. Frost, if she could speak to the class while he took roll. Dwaina had been the class leader since the first day of school, when she had told a group of loud boys to shut up so she could hear her teacher. She could be tough or funny or kind. She always seemed to know exactly what would move them.

Now Dwaina smacked both hands on her desk hard to get their attention and stood up. She pushed her glasses up onto her forehead and glared at them for a moment, hands on hips, as if she were about to lecture them:

"Okay, y'all," she began. "We've been reading about the homeless in class, and I can tell you that for some reason it's getting worse and worse." Her eyes swept around the room. "Now, my mama and I been makin' sandwiches this year till we got mayonnaise up to our elbows and we can't make enough. Why should we be up till midnight every Friday night when y'all ain't doin' a thing? Now, listen. I want you to come to my house this Friday night and help. Who'll be there?"

Twenty-three hands went up. When Dwaina excitedly reported this to her mother, Gail Brooks nearly passed out.

"Twenty-three kids? Plus *our* family?" "Yeah, Mama, isn't it great! Think how many meals we can make!"

Dwaina and Gail advised each participating family about where to get food cheaply. They made a central list of who would bring what and taped it to the refrigerator. All that week, parents drove boxes of food to the Brooks's small house. At school, the kids made bigger and bigger plans each day. Making food for the shelter was shaping up to be the social event of the year.

"Why don't y'all stay over?" asked Dwaina.

"I'll bring popcorn!" said Claire.

"I got a Hammer tape," said Qiana.

"What about boys?" said Christopher. "Can we sleep over, too?"

"Sorry," came a chorus of girls. "Oh, maybe on the kitchen floor."

The next Friday night, twenty-eight people crowded into the Brooks kitchen. They set up one of the world's longest assembly lines, kicked the radio onto 100.3 FM-JAMZ — the rap station — wrapped towels around their waists, and started in. By midnight, the boxes were filled with more than three hundred sacks.

In a little more than two years, Dwaina Brooks, now in sixth grade, has organized several thousand meals for unfortunate people in the Dallas area. She and her mother and the classmates who sometimes still join in have perfected the art of helping others and having fun at the same time. They do it by doing something they already love to do: cooking and putting meals together.

Dwaina hopes to become a doctor and open her own clinic someday, but she thinks it's crazy to wait till then to start caring for others. "Kids should get going," she says. "There aren't enough jobs out there, especially for people without diplomas. Not even at McDonald's. We should try to help. If we don't act, there will be more and more homeless people. Each of us should have some kind of concern in our hearts for other people. And we owe it, too: there isn't a one of us who hasn't been helped by someone."

BENI SEBALLOS

■ ■ ● VOLUNTEERING TO TAKE CARE OF OTHERS CAN BE JUST
AS IMPORTANT TO A COMMUNITY AS STANDING UP TO AN INJUSTICE.
IT CAN BE JUST AS CHALLENGING, TOO. BENI SEBALLOS OF RACIDA,
CALIFORNIA, OVERCAME HER SELF-DOUBT AND VOLUNTEERED TO TAKE
CARE OF OLDER PEOPLE WITH DISEASES THAT AFFECT THEIR ABILITY TO
THINK, REMEMBER, AND MOVE. THE THINGS SHE LEARNED GAVE HER
CONFIDENCE AND HELPED HER SOLVE ONE OF THE BIGGEST PROBLEMS
IN HER OWN LIFE.

One day when she was fifteen, Beni Seballos stepped
onto a plane with ten of her aunts, uncles, cousins, nieces,
and nephews and said good-bye to everything she loved.
Soon her home, her friends, and her school in the Philippines were far behind her.

When they arrived in Los Angeles, they drove to a small
house. There they would stay with her aunt and grandparents until they could find enough money to buy a home of
their own.

The fourteen of them tried their best to be cheerful. For
Beni, the hardest part was trying to get along with her
grandmother. She was a stern, quiet woman, used to the
respect that elders commanded in the Philippines. Beni was
noisy and opinionated. Her grandmother always seemed to
disapprove of her. Each day Beni would ask her grandmother if she could help with dinner, and the answer was
always no. That "no" filled the kitchen, leaving no space
for Beni. She always left the room in anger, wondering how
long she could take living there.

Racida High School was no better. She didn't know
anybody at first. She made the basketball team but rarely

got in the games. "Academic Decathlon was even worse," Beni recalls. "A team of kids from Racida High tried to answer questions faster than a team from another school. It wasn't about learning. All they wanted to do was kick butt. I hated it."

The one thing she really liked was a volunteer organization called Youth Community Services, or YCS. After hearing about it at school, Beni went on a weekend field trip to plant trees in a farm area. There was no feeling of competition here. Everyone was working together. She volunteered for YCS at a blood bank, at a recycling center, and with a program that helped keep young kids off drugs. At last, she was having fun in the United States.

Her parents didn't understand. To them, volunteering just kept her away from home. She wasn't even getting school credit for it. When Beni put on her jacket to go to a YCS event, her grandmother would glare, and her mother would say, softly but pointedly, "Oh, you're going off again, aren't you, Beni?"

During the summer break, a YCS counselor urged Beni to volunteer at a senior citizens center. The staff needed volunteers to help take care of old people who had Alzheimer's and Parkinson's diseases. Think of all you could learn, the counselor kept saying.

Beni wasn't so sure. She found herself wondering what a sixteen-year-old could really have in common with someone who was seventy-five or eighty. She hated to admit it to herself, but old people sounded boring. Even worse, what if they all treated her the way her grandmother did?

But maybe the counselor was right. After all, she thought, you learn most by doing what you understand least. Beni signed up for four days a week, five hours a day, and then walked to the library to find out about Alzheimer's and Parkinson's diseases.

A medical encyclopedia said that both diseases affect the brain's ability to function. Alzheimer's patients gradually lose their memories, and Parkinson's patients gradually lose control of their muscles. After reading less than a page, Beni

62

closed the book, unable to go on. "I was terrified," she remembers. "I could see myself having to force-feed these drooling people. I'd have to pick them up off the ground all the time. I thought they'd be vegetables.

"I practically ran out of the library. I was ready to quit before I had ever met a single patient. By the time I got home, I was wondering, 'What did I get myself into?' "

"WHAT DO YOU THINK ABOUT THIS?"

The first day, Beni introduced herself to the center's supervisor, Kathleen, and the six other volunteers, all in their forties and fifties. They were friendly, but she wondered if they really believed a teenager could handle the work.

Kathleen explained that the volunteers were supposed to feed the patients, take them for walks, and help give them their medicine. She went over each patient's medicine and diet. She kept looking at Beni and saying, "Don't worry, you'll do fine."

Then Kathleen opened the door, and they all walked out into the hallway, where about fifteen patients and their relatives were waiting. Some patients were in wheelchairs. Others were in walkers. A few leaned on canes.

Beni hung back and watched as the other volunteers rushed forward to greet the patients. Was she supposed to help them into their wheelchairs? How did you do it, anyway? What if she dropped someone? "I could see some of the patients' relatives looking at me. I felt them thinking, She's just a kid. She doesn't look like she knows what she's doing."

She followed the crowd into a big room, where the volunteers were supposed to serve the patients coffee and doughnuts. Beni's mind went blank. She couldn't remember who was supposed to have only half a doughnut and who wasn't supposed to get a doughnut at all. Kathleen was nowhere in sight. Beni fought back tears. This was terrible. It was the Alzheimer's patients who were supposed to have memory problems, not her.

After coffee, Kathleen was reading a newspaper article

to a group of patients when one of them interrupted. He pointed to Beni. "You're a young person," he said. "What do you think about this?" Beni was startled. An older person actually wanted her opinion? This was certainly different from home. Well, actually she *did* have an opinion on the topic of the article, and so she gave it. They listened carefully and discussed it. This part isn't so bad, Beni thought.

She went home that night exhausted and determined to do better tomorrow. As always, her grandmother was in the kitchen. They went through the usual routine again, with Beni offering to help and her grandmother refusing her. Beni walked out fuming. She had to get out of there.

The next morning, Beni went to the center early and memorized the patients' names. When the patients arrived, she sat down beside a frail woman named Lil with a sparse crown of thin white hair. Beni peeled an orange for her and filled up her cup of coffee halfway with a single lump of sugar, just as Lil's chart said. As she was working, Beni told Lil about what it had been like to move from the Philippines.

Lil began to talk, too. She said she had spent much of her life raising five wonderful children.

"Where are they now?" Beni asked.

"Who?"

"Your children."

"What?"

"Your children. You were saying you have five children."

Lil wrung the hem of her dress in her hands, looking frantically around the room. "What do you mean? I-I-I can't remember." She seemed to be growing more desperate by the second. Beni quickly changed the subject to her own college plans, and gradually Lil relaxed. It was Beni's first real contact with Alzheimer's disease. It taught her that she had to listen and be flexible, alert to each patient's needs. Patients wouldn't always be able to stick to the same subject for very long.

Later that week, Beni was leading a patient named Oscar outside for a game of shuffleboard when she heard the sharp scrape of metal behind her. His walker had become caught

Beni Seballos found that many of the patients she worked with enjoyed playing shuffleboard.

between two chairs. Trembling, he tried to shake loose. Beni knelt to pry the walker free, but it was no use. Oscar was growing enraged and started to shout. His face was turning red. Here it is, Beni thought, the emergency I can't handle. She sprinted into the kitchen to get help. Three volunteers and Kathy rushed out, and in a moment, they had him free. "You handled it well," Kathy said to Beni later. "Just get help."

As the summer went by, Beni faced many different kinds of challenges. A few patients tried to wander off. Some became angry because they couldn't remember when to take their medicine. One refused to go back inside after a walk.

After a few weeks at the center, Beni found herself

thinking differently about the patients. She could no longer think of them as "old people" or "senior citizens," or "Alzheimer's patients" or even "patients." They had become individuals, like her, who just happened to be at a different stage of their lives. Like her, they all had their own interests and families, hopes and fears, opinions and problems.

She discovered that if she listened carefully, she could find something in common with almost everyone. Alex wrote poetry, just like Beni. Sometimes at the shuffleboard court, they recited their poems to each other. Beni and Oscar spoke Spanish together. Blackie told her World War II stories. Mary taught her a few words of Czech. Lil loved to talk about children.

By the end of the summer, it seemed to Beni that being young had been an advantage, not a handicap, at the center. "I was special to some of the Alzheimer's patients," she says. "I think maybe having me around helped them remember how they were when they were young themselves."

BEANS AND FRIENDSHIP

In September, Beni said a tearful good-bye to the patients and staff and took a week off before school started. She had some unfinished business.

All summer long, things had gotten worse and worse with her grandmother until finally she had moved out of her aunt's house in order to find some peace in her life. But she didn't feel at peace. She loved her grandmother, and she wanted to put things right between them.

For a while it had seemed strange that she could have fun with Lil or Oscar or Alex but not her own grandmother. Then it came to her: When things got tough with a patient at the center, she kept trying patiently until she found a way to get through. But when things got tough with her grandmother, she gave up.

So one afternoon, she walked over to her aunt's house, determined to treat her grandmother as she had learned to treat the people at the center.

As usual, Beni's grandmother was in the kitchen. "Hi,"

Beni said. "Is there anything I can do?" "No," said her grandmother. This time Beni didn't leave. She noticed a bowl of string beans on the counter and carried them to the kitchen table. She sat down, picked up a bean, and snapped off the end.

She began to tell her grandmother about her summer. Though her grandmother didn't say anything, Beni could sense that she was listening. After a while, her grandmother wiped her hands on a towel, pulled up a chair, and sat down at the other end of the table. She picked up a bean and snapped the top off. A half hour later, there was a big pile of beans between them — and the beginning of a friendship.

Beni says that friendship was maybe the greatest gift of the summer. It couldn't have happened until she herself changed, and volunteering at the center was the key that opened doors within her. "The summer started working for me when I began to share myself with the patients, not just log time," she says. "Then it was fun. I know I did a good job at the center, but I probably got more out of it than the patients. I learned that caring is like a muscle. The more you exercise it, the more you *can* share."

I FEEL MYSELF
   GROW OLD
MY EYES GO BLIND
   MY HANDS SHAKE
PLEASE, LORD, LET
   SOMEONE ALSO
   HELP ME OUT
WHEN TOMORROW'S DAWNS
   GROW DARK ON
   ME.
           — BENI SEBALLOS

JAMES ALE

▲ ■ ● **WHEN HE WAS NINE, JAMES ALE SAW HIS FRIEND GET HIT BY A CAR WHEN THEY WERE PLAYING BALL IN A CROWDED STREET. IT MADE HIM WONDER, WHY SHOULD THEY HAVE TO PLAY IN THE STREET WHEN KIDS IN THE RICH PART OF TOWN HAD PARKS? THE MORE HE THOUGHT, THE MADDER HE GOT. FINALLY, JAMES ALE TOOK ON TOWN HALL.**

James Ale cried out as his friend Bobby Adams settled into position to catch the ball. Bobby was concentrating so hard that he didn't hear the white Thunderbird as it tore around the corner, heading toward him. He was on the ground, his leg bent in pain, before he even knew what happened.

James and his friends live in Davie, Florida, on the edge of the Everglades. Davie is really two towns. The western part is where rich people from Miami build ranches and keep their horses. The eastern part, where James and Bobby live, is a neighborhood of small trailers and condominiums on tiny lots.

At the time Bobby Adams was hit by the car, their neighborhood was full of children who had no place to play but in the street. At night, kids crawled around on Dumpsters left in front of construction sites. The nearest park was across a highway. You took your life in your hands every time you tried to get there. James's parents wouldn't let him even try.

As the sound of Bobby's ambulance faded into the distance, James walked slowly home. He was angry. Bobby wouldn't have gotten hurt if they had a park to play in. But officials never spent any money in this part of town.

James looked over at a small worn field right behind the water plant. That would be a perfect place for a park.

There could be a playground at one end for the little kids and a basketball court at the other end. And some lights. Everyone would use it.

In that moment, James decided to make it happen. He'd organize the kids, and they'd beat down the mayor's door. They'd call themselves Children for Davie. So what if he was only nine?

That evening, James asked his dad for advice. As president of the local condominium association, John Ale was always going off to the town council meetings. If anyone would know how to pressure Davie's government, his dad would.

John Ale listened carefully to his son's idea before speaking. "You'll have to know exactly what you want and be able to prove that it's important. Playground equipment will cost money, and people ask the mayor and the town council for money every day," he said. "Everyone thinks their project is the most important thing in the world, and there's only so much tax money to go around."

Father and son sat together in silence. "But you can do it," Mr. Ale said. "More than anything, you'll have to be persistent. You can't quit."

PREPARING FOR ACTION

James decided to start at the top. The next day, he telephoned the mayor.

"Mayor Kovac's office," said a pleasant voice.

"May I talk to the mayor?"

"She's not in. May I take a message?"

James left his name and telephone number. A few hours later, the mayor called him back. "I told her what had happened to Bobby Adams and said we needed a park in our neighborhood," James recalls. "I could tell she wasn't paying much attention. She seemed to be in a hurry. All she said was that she'd look into it and call me back.

"A while later she did. She said once there had been a park in our area and it had been vandalized. It was like we had blown our only chance. Then she didn't say anything.

Finally I just said, 'Well, I think we need a park,' and we hung up. I felt discouraged. She treated me like a kid. I had to get her to pay attention."

James went to his room, flicked on his computer, and typed *Children for Davie* in bold print at the top of the screen. Below that, he typed out a petition calling for a new park. "Please sign this if you think that it would be better for our neighborhood if there were a park," it concluded. Beneath that he put blanks for signatures.

He printed it out, snapped it onto a clipboard, and went outside to try to get kids to sign it. They squinted at his petition, then looked at him as if he were crazy.

"Sure, man, *you're* gonna get us a park."

"Well, don't you think we need one? Look what happened to Bobby."

"Yeah, we need one, but who's gonna listen to *you?*"

"Not just me. We'll all go. She'll have to listen to all of us."

"You're outa your mind." They were starting to drift away.

"Well, just sign it if you're for it, okay?"

James got fifty kids to sign, but no one would go with him to see the mayor, not even Bobby Adams, who by now was back from the hospital and recovering from a broken leg.

James called the mayor again, this time asking for an appointment to talk about the park in person. She said yes. James prepared carefully for that meeting. Above all, he needed to be taken seriously. Here's what he did:

▲ *He gathered more signatures on his petition.*
■ *He took a map of Davie and outlined the site where he wanted the park, so the mayor would know just where it should be.*
● *He typed out a letter on his Children for Davie stationery to leave with the mayor, listing the reasons why the park should be built and stating exactly what the town should provide: swings, a slide, monkey bars, a basketball court, and lights.*
▲ *He made up some business cards on his computer. They said, "James Ale, President, Children for Davie."*

On the afternoon of the meeting, James put on his red suit jacket, a red shirt, and gray pants and squeezed into his hard black shoes. He combed his hair carefully. "When the time came for my mom to pick me up and drive me over there, I was ready."

"IT SHOULD BE HERE."

Mayor Joan Kovac had expected James Ale to be a child who maybe wanted to tell his friends he had met the mayor in person. But the boy who walked through the door had business on his mind. "He came in with a briefcase," she recalls. "And then he handed me a business card."

CHILDREN FOR DAVIE

JAMES ALE
Director   792-7758

Looking directly at her, James told the mayor that his neighborhood was unsafe for kids. They had no place to play. They needed a park. It would help the town, he said, because it would save lives. The crime rate would go down because kids would have something to do. Mayor Kovac was leaning forward, looking right at him and listening carefully. When he finished, she got up and walked around her desk to a map of Davie. She pointed to three dots, clustered together on the west side of town.

"We're building three new parks right now, James," she said. "Can't your parents take you to one of them?"

"No," said James. "My parents both work. So do every-one else's around me. Those parks are a long way from us. We need a place of our own."

The mayor looked at the map again. "But there's no empty land where you live. Everything's all built up. Do you have a suggestion?"

James pulled the map from his briefcase and spread it on the mayor's desk. "It should be here," he said, pointing to the square he had drawn. "Behind the water plant. It's the right place. Look at this petition from the kids in the neighborhood. Everyone agrees."

Mayor Kovac had no choice but to respect him. He wasn't criticizing her or blaming the town. He had come to her with a plan. He was representing a group, and he wanted her support. She had to consider his proposal.

"Well," she said at last, "let me talk to some people in the Parks Department. We'll have to visit the site. I can't make any promises now, but I can promise I won't just put you off.''

James got up and extended his hand, smiling. He pointed to his card on her desk. ''My phone number is right here,'' he said. ''I look forward to hearing from you.''

"WE'RE GOING TO BUILD THAT KID A PARK."

One Saturday morning a few weeks later, James met the mayor and the town administrator behind the water tower. James had been studying up on how Davie's government worked. The mayor and the town administrator were Davie's two most important officials. Along with the town attorney and the five members of the town council, they made the big decisions on how to run Davie's business. The town administrator did most of the detailed, day-to-day business.

James had gone to meet with him, too. He was a nice enough man — he had even given James tickets to a wrestling meet — but he didn't seem very interested in the park. Still, he had agreed to visit the site. Now James had the town's two most important people together right where he wanted them. This was his chance.

First James pointed to the spot where Bobby Adams had been hit. Several kids were running around. They had to agree that it would be hard for a turning car to see them.

Then James walked them around the small field. ''This is the perfect place for us,'' James said. The administrator frowned. The lot was too small for a park, he said. He advised James to be patient. Someday the town would tear down a couple of houses and build the kids a real park.

''We don't want to wait for a bigger park,'' James said flatly. ''We need this park, here and now. This is the right place. It will get used. You already own the land, and we're just talking about playground equipment. We're not asking for much.'' He could see the man's mind was closed.

If they thought James Ale would go away, they were

wrong. He waited a few days for an answer, and when none came, he tried even harder. Nearly every day after school, he wrote brief, carefully worded letters to town officials. He also sent them updated copies of his ever-growing petition.

One night he called the secretary assigned to the town council and asked if, representing Children for Davie, he could speak briefly to the council members at Wednesday night's meeting.

"Are you a voter?" the secretary asked.

"Well, no, but I —"

"Then the answer is no," she said firmly.

James turned up the heat. He called the reporter for a Miami newspaper assigned to Davie and offered him the story of a young boy taking on town hall for the kids in his neighborhood. The reporter accepted, and a story soon appeared in the newspaper. James sent a copy to town officials.

Every few days, he called Mayor Kovac and asked her for a progress report. He was always polite. Did she need any more information? Was there anything he could do to help?

Finally his work paid off. One evening after school, James was surprised to receive a call from the town council's secretary inviting him to a council meeting. The next Wednesday evening, Mayor Kovac announced the creation of a new park. Asking him to stand, she introduced James by saying, "This boy could teach a lot of adults I know a few things about lobbying town government."

Mayor Kovac says that the small area that everyone in Davie now calls James Ale Park has become the most popular playground site in Davie. "I drive by it, and there are never fewer than thirty kids there," she says. "The parks we built in the richer parts of town are barely used. James was right."

The kids in the neighborhood thought it was a miracle that a nine-year-old boy actually got his town to spend five thousand dollars to build a park for them. But it wasn't a miracle. He simply used tried-and-true lobbying techniques.

▲ ▲ ● ▬▬▬
"THIS KID COULD TEACH A LOT OF ADULTS I KNOW HOW TO LOBBY ELECTED OFFICIALS. HE JUST DIDN'T GIVE UP."
—MAYOR JOAN KOVAC, DAVIE, FLORIDA
▬▬▬ ● ■ ■

In Mayor Kovac's words:

● *James went right to the person who had power — me, in this case — and got to know me. It was smart, because lobbying is partly personal. I like James.* ▲ *He came with a very specific plan. He had it in writing so that I could show it to people.* ■ *His petition showed that he was representing other children.* ● *He was able to say, in a very few words, why that park was needed. And I could tell he really believed in it.* ▲ *He didn't come with a budget — probably he should have — but he knew what he wanted at the park. That made it easy for me to figure out the cost.* ■ *He was always available to meet officials at the site. He provided information that we needed. He was on time.* ● *He was respectful. He kept pressure on us without being obnoxious or turning us off. And he listened to me.* ▲ *He was persistent. That's the most important thing of all. He just never gave up. I don't think he ever would have.* ■ *One other thing. He paid me back, and in the right way. When my campaign for reelection came up, James called and asked if he could help. He went door-to-door asking people to vote for me. I mean he really blitzed that neighborhood. He was an asset to me. During the campaign, I listed the creation of James Ale Park as one of my major accomplishments.*

On the day the park James Ale fought for was dedicated, one admiring friend said, "He has done a lot of things for us. He has a lot of courage."

And what did James learn? "I learned a lot. People in government will tell a kid that they don't have time for little things like a park," James says. "But if you think about it, it really is a big thing. I had a good idea and I never gave up. Kids have rights, too. But we have to learn to use them."

74

HEALING
THE
EARTH

WE DON'T INHERIT THE LAND FROM OUR ANCESTORS. WE BORROW IT FROM OUR CHILDREN.

— PENNSYLVANIA DUTCH SAYING

ANDREW HOLLEMAN

■▲■● **Twelve-year-old Andrew Holleman fought
for nearly a year to keep the forest he loved from being
destroyed by a developer. Much was at stake: habitat for at
least three endangered species, the source of his town's
water, and the place he loved more than anywhere on earth.
To succeed, he had to get smart — and get help — fast.**

One afternoon in late August, Andrew Holleman's mother stood at the table reading a letter that had just come in the mail. She seemed upset. "What is it, Mom?" he asked. Shaking her head, she passed it to Andrew.

Andrew's eyes narrowed. It was from a company whose president was announcing that he wanted to develop the private land next to Andrew's yard. The developer wanted to build 180 condominium units.

Andrew was stunned. He had loved and studied and explored that land ever since he could remember. Each summer, he pulled bass from the stream that ran through it. Every winter, he played hockey on the frozen stream with his friends. Using their field guides, he and a friend had learned to identify nearly all the plants and animals that lived there. Andrew especially liked to follow the stream back to a flat rock, where he would sit, whittling and thinking. From that rock he had seen deer and foxes pass by. Once a red-tailed hawk had settled onto a snag about ten feet away and stared at him, cocking its head as if it were trying to figure out what sort of creature Andrew was. The thought of losing all that was unbearable.

76

Andrew looked at the letter's final sentence. His parents were invited to an open meeting at town hall to hear the developer describe his plans. The meeting was only four weeks away. Sitting at his kitchen table, Andrew went through a kind of metamorphosis. His initial shock melted into anger, and then the anger changed into a cold determination. Somehow Andrew Holleman was going to stop that development.

"ARE YOU STILL LOOKING?"

Andrew needed information, fast. He knew there were laws in Massachusetts, where he lived, that said when you could and couldn't put buildings on wetlands. And most of the land next door was wet all the time.

His mother dropped him off at the library, and soon Andrew was staring at bookcases full of Massachusetts law books. He needed to find the Hatch Act, which his parents had told him was the law that controlled the development of wetlands in Massachusetts.

Two hours later, Andrew's mother returned to find him barely visible behind a mountain of law books. She picked out a book of her own and sat down. A few minutes later, she heard him shout. Several nearby readers looked up. "Finally I found it," Andrew remembers. "It was clear: The Hatch Act said it was illegal to build within one hundred feet of a wetland unless you had a permit.

"I asked the librarian what else I should read. She reached behind her desk and handed me the master plan for my town, Chelmsford." A master plan is a guide to the way all the land in a town can be used. It tells which land can be developed for industry, which land can support houses or apartments, and which must be left open for parks or nature areas.

Quickly he found the land by his house on a map that came with the plan. "I could see that the developer wanted to develop 16.3 acres; that's how big the site was. But 8.5 acres were zoned as wetlands and 5.6 of the rest were considered to be poor soil. It looked like only 2.2 acres were considered developable."

Weary but happy, Andrew got up from his desk and pulled on his jacket. Now he had the ammunition he needed.

"PLEASE SIGN THE ATTACHED SHEET."

Andrew knew the developer's plan was probably illegal, but that didn't mean anyone else knew, or that anyone else would care. He needed a way to educate people about the developer's plan and its weaknesses before the meeting.

He decided to write a petition opposing the development and ask the registered voters who lived in the neighborhood to sign it. He could then send copies to local politicians. If they could see that most voters were against the development, Andrew reasoned, they might be persuaded.

The petition had to be short and to the point. "I knew it couldn't be more than a page long, because people tend to ignore longer things," he says. "I gave basic information about the site and the law. Then I said, 'If you agree with me that this land shouldn't be developed, please sign the attached sheet.' "

Every night for the next few weeks, Andrew raced home from school, did his homework, bolted down dinner, and then headed out to gather signatures. He was very patient. "Some nights I would be out for two hours and I'd get only five signatures, because people would bring me into their house and offer me cookies while they discussed it with me. That was fine with me. I didn't want to get in a hurry and leave out information. I wanted to make sure I had a chance to answer every question they could think of."

Andrew also created a petition at school. Even though they couldn't vote, he hoped his schoolmates would want to add their voices to the fight. "Some kids didn't agree with me, but the majority did. I just kept on going."

And he continued his research. He called the state Audubon Society's Environmental Health Line and asked for ideas. Dr. Dorothy Arvison, a staff biologist, told him how to get a list of the state's endangered and threatened species from the Massachusetts Division of Fisheries and Wildlife.

When the list arrived in the mail, Andrew recognized three species — the wood turtle, the yellow salamander, and the great blue heron — that lived on his land. He remembered that one day he had found a wood turtle shell in an old trap. He had picked it up and taken it back to his room. The list gave him an idea for how that old shell could be useful. He thought the turtle would approve.

ORGANIZING AN AMBUSH

As the night of the meeting approached, Andrew went over his list of things to do. A neighbor had already contacted some reporters, who had said they'd be there. Andrew had written letters to newspaper editors opposing the development. The petition now had over 180 signatures, and there was no one left to visit. He had sent copies to town officials and to his state senators and representatives.

Finally he wrote a speech to give at the meeting. Every night after his homework, Andrew gathered his parents, his brother, and sister and asked them to help him rehearse.

He opened by saying how much he loved the land. He said it provided a home for three endangered species. He said that the sewage from so much development would poison the local groundwater — and Chelmsford's wells, the town's drinking water. He even proposed an alternative site for development: the old drive-in theater. Raising the wood turtle's shell aloft and shaking it at his family, Andrew ended by listing all the reasons why the developer's proposal should be rejected. "Well?" Andrew would ask his family, totally inspired. "What do you think?" "Speak more slowly," his brother would suggest. "How about doing it one more time?" his mother would add.

When it came time to leave for the meeting, Andrew felt the calmness and confidence that comes with having prepared carefully. He had been organizing almost nonstop for a month. The trap was set, and Andrew was ready.

▲ ▲ ● ▬▬▬

"BELIEVE IT OR NOT, WHEN YOU'RE YOUNG, YOU MIGHT HAVE A BETTER CHANCE THAN WHEN YOU ARE AN ADULT. IT'S MUCH RARER FOR A KID TO OPPOSE A DEVELOPMENT THAN AN ADULT. I THINK PEOPLE MIGHT TEND TO LISTEN MORE TO A KID."
— ANDREW HOLLEMAN

▬▬▬ ● ■ ■

"Where Did All These People Come From?"

At 7:30, the developer and town officials watched in amazement as hundreds of Chelmsford residents lined up outside the town hall. The developer had sent letters to only fifty nearby residents. Where had all these people come from? And where were they going to put them all? First they changed rooms to the selectmen's office but even then the crowd spilled out into the hall. Finally a town official begged the girls' high school basketball coach to end practice early and let them have the gym. By 8:00, there were over 250 people in the bleachers.

The developer began by presenting his plan and then asked if anyone wanted to speak. Andrew rose and walked slowly to the front of the room, carrying his note cards and the turtle shell. There was applause, and then quiet.

Andrew's speech went perfectly. The only surprise came when Andrew suggested the developer build instead at the site of the old drive-in movie theater. "I found out the guy had already started a condominium there."

▲ ■ ● "It's been said that we don't inherit our land from our parents — we borrow it from our children. That's the attitude you have to take. You're a child; it's your land. You're gonna be around a lot longer than these adults; you have more reason to care. Why not fight for it? They'll ruin your chance if they screw up your future. It's our earth. I challenge kids to protect it. If we don't do it, no one else is going to."—Andrew Holleman

The struggle was far from over. Although now it was clear that most neighbors opposed the development, the developer wasn't about to give up. Over the next ten months, he presented his plans to the conservation commission, zoning board, appeals board, and selectmen. They all had to say yes for his plan to go through. Andrew was determined to help them say no.

"I went to every meeting, usually with my parents," Andrew remembers. "Sometimes I went to two or three meetings a week. Usually they were on school nights, and often I didn't get home until eleven. My mother kept saying, 'Don't get burned out; if you need to stop now, it's okay — you've already made a good try.' "

Because they were together so much, Andrew came to know the developer. Although he hated the man's plan, he didn't hate the man himself. "It's like how lawyers can be fighting tooth and nail in a courtroom one minute and then be friendly out in the hall," Andrew says. "That's the way we were. When it was time for business, we got down to business."

The developer seemed to respect Andrew as a worthy opponent, even if he was young — although once, in a meeting, he hollered, "I'm not going to discuss hydro-geological information with a twelve-year-old!" "He was really worked up," Andrew recalls. "I didn't take it personally."

Together with a few neighbors, Andrew's parents formed a neighborhood association and went door-to-door asking for money to hire a lawyer and a scientist to testify at hearings. They ended up raising $16,000.

Dr. Arvidson, the Audubon biologist, never seemed to run out of ideas for Andrew. Once, while she was giving him a long list of suggestions, Andrew interrupted. "Hey, I'm only twelve years old," he told her. "That's no excuse," she said, and went right on talking.

VICTORY!

Finally it came time to test whether the soil at the site could hold the enormous amount of sewage — dishwater, bath water, toilet water, water from washing machines — that would be created in 180 condominiums.

While Andrew, his father, and several town officials watched, the developer fired up a backhoe and dug about fifteen deep holes in the soil. Muddy water quickly filled all the holes but two and then spilled out onto the grass. That meant sewage from the proposed condominiums would flow right down into drinking water. The plan had failed the test.

Two weeks later, the zoning board of appeals met to make a final decision. The developer, sensing that he was about to lose, asked to withdraw his application. That way he would be able to try again, for fewer condominiums. But the board ruled that the site was simply not suitable for development. Andrew had won!

When the zoning board gave its ruling, Andrew felt like shattering the hearing room with a mighty whoop, but instead, he walked over and shook the developer's hand. No reason to burn bridges, he told himself.

Now Andrew is hard at work with his ultimate plan, which is to convince the town to buy the land and use it as a nature preserve. He won't rest until the land he loves is absolutely safe. "If I don't do it," he says, "no one else is going to."

Andrew Holleman in the forest he saved from a developer's bulldozer.

82

FOUNDERS
OF THE CHILDREN'S
RAIN FOREST

▲ ■ ● **FORTY FIRST- AND SECOND-GRADE STUDENTS FROM A SMALL SCHOOL IN SWEDEN BECAME UPSET WHEN THEIR TEACHER TOLD THEM THAT RAIN FORESTS WERE BEING DESTROYED RAPIDLY THROUGHOUT THE WORLD. THEY WONDERED WHAT THEY — SO YOUNG, SO FEW, AND SO FAR AWAY FROM THE TROPICS — COULD DO THAT COULD REALLY MATTER. THEIR ANSWER HAS HELPED PRESERVE RAIN FORESTS AROUND THE WORLD.**

It all began in the first week of school when Eha Kern, from the Fagervik School, in the Swedish countryside, showed her forty first- and second-grade students pictures of hot, steamy jungles near the Equator. It was there, she said, that half the types of plants and animals in the whole world could be found. She read to them about monkeys and leopards and sloths, about snakes that can paralyze your nerves with one bite, about strange plants that might hold a cure for cancer, about the great trees that give us oxygen to breathe and help keep the earth from becoming too hot.

And then she told them that the world's rain forests were being destroyed at the rate of one hundred acres a *minute*. In the past thirty years, she said, nearly half the world's rain forests have been cut down, often by poor people who burn the wood for fire. Sometimes forests are cleared to make pastures for cattle that are slaughtered and sold to hamburger chains in the U.S. and Europe. Sometimes the trees are sold and shipped away to make furniture and paper. More often they are just stacked up and burned. At this rate, there might not be any rain forests left in thirty years!

The children were horrified. The creatures of the rain forest could be gone before the students were even old enough to have a chance to see them. It didn't matter that they lived thousands of miles away in cold, snowy Sweden. It seemed to them that their future was being chopped and cleared away.

During the autumn, as the sunlight weakened and the days became short, the Fagervik children continued to think about the rain forest. Whenever they went on walks past the great fir trees on the school grounds, they imagined jaguars crouched in the limbs just above them, their long tails twitching impatiently.

They begged Mrs. Kern to help them think of something — anything — they could do to rescue the creatures of the tropics. And then one afternoon during a music lesson, a student named Roland Tiensuu asked suddenly, "Can't we just *buy* some rain forest?"

The lesson stopped. It was a simple, clear idea that all the others understood at once. The class began to cheer, and then they turned to their teacher. "Please, Mrs. Kern," they said. "Please, won't you find us a forest to buy?"

"Please Buy Mine."

Mrs. Kern had no idea how to find a rain forest for sale. But then, the very weekend after Roland's idea, she was introduced to an American biologist named Sharon Kinsman. As they chatted, Ms. Kinsman explained that she had been working in a rain forest called Monte Verde, or Green Mountain.

When Mrs. Kern told Ms. Kinsman of the nearly impossible mission her students had given her, she expected the biologist to laugh. Instead her expression turned serious. "Oh," she said quickly, "please buy mine."

▲ ▲ ● ■■■■■

"Only within the moment of time represented by the present century has one species — man — acquired significant power to alter the nature of the world."
— Rachel Carson,
Silent Spring, 1962

■■■■ ● ■ ■

84

WHY ARE RAIN FORESTS IMPORTANT?

▲ By the time it is one hundred years old, one rain forest tree has provided enough oxygen for a human being to breathe for twenty years.

■ More than one-quarter of the medicinal drugs prescribed in the United States come from rain forest plants.

● Most of the plants that have cancer-fighting properties grow in tropical rain forests.

▲ Though tropical rain forests cover only a small part of the earth, half the world's plants and animal species are found within them.

■ Many foods come from rain forests. When your parents drink coffee or you eat chocolate, you are consuming the products of the rain forest.

● Rain forests act as giant sponges, absorbing and recycling rainwater. Without rain forests, there would be more floods and droughts, and the deserts of the world would expand.

Ms. Kinsman said that some people in Monte Verde were trying desperately to buy land so that more trees wouldn't be cut. Much land had already been protected, but much more was needed. Land was cheap there, she said — only about twenty-five dollars per acre.

Ms. Kinsman agreed to visit the Fagervik School. She would bring a map and slides of the Monte Verde forest and tell the children where they could send money to buy rain forest land. When Mrs. Kern told the children what had happened, they didn't even seem surprised. As they put it, "We knew you would find one."

"THERE ARE NO BAD IDEAS."

In the days before Sharon Kinsman's visit, the Fagervik students began to think about how to raise money. They asked Mrs. Kern to write down all their ideas. As she picked up a piece of chalk, several children spoke at once.

"Pony rides!"

"Let's collect old things and sell them!"

"What about a rain forest evening here at school?"

"Dog washing!"

Dog washing? They began to laugh. "That would never work," someone said. "Who would give money for that?" Mrs. Kern put her chalk down. "Look," she said. "Let's make this our rule: there are no bad ideas. The only bad thing is if you have an idea and don't say it. Then we can't use it." She returned to the blackboard. Were there more ideas?

"A rabbit jumping contest!"

"Rabbit jumping?" said Mrs. Kern. "Be serious. You can't *make* a rabbit jump."

"Oh, yes, we all have rabbits. We can train them. We can. We *can!*"

Mrs. Kern tried to imagine someone actually paying money to watch children try to make rabbits jump. She couldn't. This idea was crazy.

"Mrs. Kern . . . there's no such thing as a bad idea . . . remember?" She did. "Rabbit jumping," she wrote, dutifully putting her doubts aside.

GIANT SPIDERS AND DEADLY SNAKES

On November 6, 1987, Sharon Kinsman arrived at the Fagervik School. She was just as enthusiastic as the students. They put on skits for her about rain forests and showed her the many books they had written about tropical creatures. Then at last, it was her turn to show them slides of the Monte Verde forest.

First she unfolded a map of the forest and pointed to the area their money could preserve from cutting. She told them that 400 bird species live in the forest, more than in all of Sweden, as well as 490 kinds of butterflies and 500 types

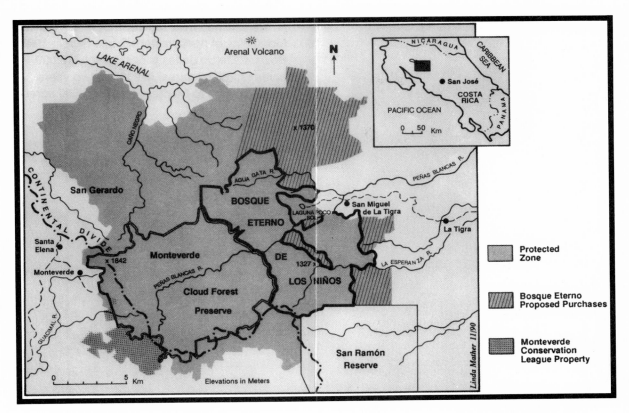

Here is a map of the Children's Rain Forest.

of trees. Monte Verde is also the only home in the world, she said, for the golden toad, a creature that seems to glow in the dark.

Then she showed her slides. As the room became dark, the students were swept into a hot, steamy jungle half the world away. The slides took them sloshing along a narrow, muddy trail, crisscrossed with roots and vines. A dark canopy of giant trees, thick with bright flowering plants, closed in above them.

They saw giant spiders and deadly snakes. Ms. Kinsman's tape recorder made the forest ring with the shriek of howler monkeys calling to each other and with the chattering of parrots above the trees. They saw the golden toad, the scarlet macaw, and the red-backed poison-arrow frog.

And they saw the forest disappearing, too. They saw hard-muscled men, their backs glistening with sweat, pushing chain saws deep into the giant trees. They could almost

▲ ▲ ● ▬▬▬▬

"THE FROG DOES NOT DRINK UP THE POND IN WHICH IT LIVES."
— BUDDHIST PROVERB

▬▬▬▬ ● ■ ■

smell the smoke of burning tree limbs and feel the thunder of thick, brown trunks crashing down. Behind great piles of ragged wood, the tropical sky was hazy with smoke. Time seemed very short.

When the lights came on, the students were back in Sweden, but they were not the same. Now they had seen their forest — and the danger it faced. There was no time to lose. Mrs. Kern had inspired them with a problem, and Roland had given them an idea they could work with. Sharon Kinsman had shown them their target. Now it was up to them.

"WE KNEW WHAT WE WANTED."

Two weeks later, more than a hundred people crowded into an old schoolhouse near the Fagervik School for a rain forest evening. Students stood by the door and collected ten crowns (about $1.50) from each person. Special programs cost another crown. Even though it was winter, rain splattered steadily onto the roof, just as it must have been raining in the Monte Verde forest. To the students, rain was a good sign.

Here are the children from the Fagervik School in Sweden who started a multimillion-dollar effort to preserve rain forest habitats for endangered plants and animals.

First they performed a play containing a dramatic scene in which trees of the rain forest were cut and creatures killed. That way guests would understand the problem they were trying to help solve. As the applause died down, the children passed an old hat around, urging audience members to drop money in it.

Then they sold rain forest books and rain forest poems. "We were not afraid to ask for money," remembers Maria Karlsson, who was nine. "We knew what we wanted was important." One boy stood at a table keeping track of how much they were making. Whenever a classmate would hand over a fresh delivery of cash, he would count it quickly and shout above the noise, "Now we've got two hundred crowns!!" "Now it's three hundred!!"

The evening's total came to 1,600 crowns, or about $240. The next day, they figured out that they had raised enough money to save about twelve football fields worth of rain forest. It was wonderful . . . but was it enough space for a sloth? A leopard? They all knew the answer. They needed more.

They filled up another blackboard with ideas and tried them out. Everything seemed to work. Mrs. Kern brought in a list of prominent people who might make donations. Two girls wrote a letter to the richest woman on the list. A few days later, a check arrived. Someone else wrote to the king of Sweden and asked if he would watch them perform plays about the rain forest. He said yes.

One day they went to a recording studio and made a tape of their rain forest songs. From the very beginning, Mrs. Kern and a music teacher had been helping them write songs. They started with old melodies they liked, changing them a little as they went along. As soon as anybody came up with a good line, they sang it into a tape recorder so they wouldn't forget it by the end of the song. They rehearsed the songs many times on their school bus before recording them, then designed a cover and used some of their money to buy plastic boxes for the tapes. Within months, they had sold five hundred tapes at ten dollars each.

The more they used their imaginations, the more money

The children of the Fagervik School designed their own invitations to rain forest fundraising events.

The Fagervik students also made their own tape and sold hundreds of copies to raise money for the Children's Rain Forest.

89

they raised. They decided to have a fair. "We had a magician and charged admission," remembers Lia Degeby, who was eight. "We charged to see who could make the ugliest face. We had a pony riding contest. We had a market. We had a lady with a beard. We had the strongest lady in the world. Maria forecast the future in a cabin. We tried everything." The biggest money maker of all was the rabbit jumping contest, even though each rabbit sat still when its time came to jump! Even carrots couldn't budge them. One simply flopped over and went to sleep, crushing its necklace of flowers.

Soon they needed a place to put all the money they had earned. Mrs. Kern's husband, Bernd, helped them form an organization called Barnens Regnskog, which means Children's Rain Forest. They opened a bank account with a post office box where people could continue to mail donations.

By midwinter, they had raised $1,400. The children addressed an envelope to the Monte Verde Cloud Forest Protection League, folded a check inside, and sent it on its way to Costa Rica. Weeks later, they received a crumpled package covered with brightly colored stamps. It contained a map of the area that had been bought with their money. A grateful writer thanked them for saving nearly ninety acres of Costa Rican rain forest.

In the early spring, the Fagervik students performed at the Swedish Children's Fair, which led to several national television appearances. Soon schools from all over Sweden were joining Barnens Regnskog and sending money to Monte Verde. At one high school near Stockholm, two thousand students did chores all day in the city and raised nearly $15,000. And inspired by the students, the Swedish government gave a grant of $80,000 to Monte Verde.

Roy Vargas Garcia.

"I THINK OF MY FUTURE."

After another year's work, the children of Fagervik had raised $25,000 more. The families who could afford it sent their children to Costa Rica to see Monte Verde. Just before Christmas, ten Fagervik children stepped off the plane,

A Letter From a Boy of the Monte Verde Rain Forest

My name is Roy Vargas Garcia. I am twelve years old. I live in a small community called La Cruz de Abangares, in Costa Rica. There are seven in my family. My father is a dairyman, my mother a housewife.

I love to listen to the songs of birds and insects of the forest. Often I see sloths, gray foxes, armadillos, opossums, birds, monkeys, and butterflies. The climate here is cool, and trees are tall and green, with many mosses.

I am very pleased that other children from around the world want to protect our forest. I want children to know that we who live here are protecting it, too.

In the past, our farmers cut the forest. Not because they did not care about it, but because they needed to make their farms and their vegetable gardens and to get firewood and lumber and so to raise their children.

But now many farmers are planting trees in windbreaks on the farms. In my community we are buying a small piece of land we call a community reserve to protect where our water comes from. We are doing this with help and training from the Monte Verde Conservation League.

I want to thank all the children who are helping save forests. Thank you.

Roy Vargas Garcia

---

blinking in the bright Costa Rican sunlight. It was hot! They stripped off their coats and sweaters, piled into a bus, and headed for the mountains.

A few hours later, the bus turned onto a narrow, rocky road that threaded its way through steep mountains. The children looked out upon spectacular waterfalls that fell hundreds of feet. Occasionally they glimpsed monkeys swinging through the trees.

Ahead, the mountaintops disappeared inside a dark

purple cloud. For a few moments they could see five rainbows at once. Soon it began to rain.

The next morning, they joined ten Costa Rican children and went on a hike through the Monte Verde rain forest. Sometimes the thick mud made them step right out of their boots. But it didn't matter. "There were plants everywhere," says Lia. "I saw monkeys and flowers."

On Christmas day, the children of the Fagervik School proudly presented the staff of the Monte Verde Cloud Forest with their check for $25,000. They said it was a holiday present for all the children of the world.

The Monte Verde Conservation League used their gift, and funds that had been donated by other children previously, to establish what is now known as El Bosque Eterno de los Ninos, or the Eternal International Children's Rain Forest. It is a living monument to the caring and power of young people everywhere. So far, kids from twenty-one nations have raised more than two million dollars to preserve nearly 33,000 acres of rain forest, plenty of room for jaguars and ocelots and tapirs. The first group of Fagervik students have now graduated to another school, but the first- and second-graders who have replaced them are still raising great sums of money. The school total is now well over $50,000.

▲ ▲ ● ▬▬▬▬
"CHILDREN ARE THE WEALTH OF THE WORLD."
— ARAB SAYING
▬▬▬▬ ● ■ ■

The Fagervik students continue to amaze their teacher. "I never thought they could do so much," Mrs. Kern says. "Sometimes I say to them, 'Why do you work so hard?' They say, 'I think of my future.' They make me feel optimistic. When I am with them, I think maybe anything can be done.' "

You, too, can enlarge the Children's Rain Forest. To find out how, write to:

The Children's Rain Forest
P.O. Box 936
Lewiston, Maine 04240

or:

The Monte Verde Conservation League
Apartido 10165-1000
San José, Costa Rica

The Monte Verde Conservation League accepts checks in American dollars; say that you want your gift to go to the Children's Rain Forest. At this address you can also find out how to contact groups from each nation belonging to the International Children's Rain Forest Network. Donations are tax deductible at either address.

This huge forest, El Bosque Eterno de los Ninos, in Monte Verde, Costa Rica, was saved from destruction through money raised by children around the world.

JOEL RUBIN

▲ ■ ● JOEL RUBIN, FIFTEEN, FOUND A WAY TO INFLUENCE A HUGE MULTINATIONAL CORPORATION TO CHANGE THE WAY IT CATCHES TUNA IN THE PACIFIC OCEAN IN ORDER TO KEEP DOLPHINS FROM BEING KILLED. HIS STRATEGY WAS DIRECT, PERSONAL, AND HARD-HITTING. AS HE PUT IT, "YOU DON'T ALWAYS HAVE TO BE POLITE."

One Sunday afternoon, Joel Rubin, a fifteen-year-old tenth-grader from Cape Elizabeth, Maine, slumped into a chair in the family rec room and snapped on the TV. He flipped around on the cable channels for a while, then locked onto a show about dolphins.

At first there were scenes of dolphins in family groups. They seemed amazingly like humans: intelligent, friendly, and playful. Through something like radar, they beamed out sounds that let them talk to one another.

Then the scene changed to a large tuna fishing boat in the eastern Pacific. The boat was specially equipped with large drift nets to haul in hundreds of tuna at once. The narrator said that dolphins and yellowfin tuna swim together. The dolphins swim above the tuna, leaping out of the water from time to time to breathe. That makes them perfect markers for tuna fishers.

"The tuna ship sent out helicopters to spot dolphins," Joel remembers. "Then the pilot would radio back to the ship, and suddenly speedboats would zoom out to surround the dolphins. They wanted to make the dolphins stay in one place so the tuna below wouldn't move. That way they could get nets around all the tuna."

As Joel watched, horrified, boat pilots hurled small bombs at the male dolphins who led the group and tried to run over them with their boat propellers. The sea was soon smeared with blood. The tuna ship steamed into the picture, and fishermen on deck hurriedly cast out a mile-long net. One edge was held up on the surface by a line of floats, while the other edge sunk down several hundred feet into the water.

The workers on the tuna boat closed up the net by cranking cables, as if they were pulling the drawstrings on a giant purse. Underwater cameras showed dolphins, trapped among hundreds of tuna, frantically trying to thrash their way out of the net before they ran out of oxygen. Then the giant net, bulging with writhing fish and dolphins, was hoisted high above the ship and dropped about forty feet down onto the deck. It landed with a crash that shook the camera.

Joel sank back into his chair. He had never been an emotional person, but now he was nearly paralyzed with shock. "Those pictures did something to me," he remembers. "I had never felt that way before. It was the most disgusting thing I had ever seen. I had never tried to change anything before, but I had to do something about this."

WHAT COULD ONE STUDENT DO?

In the winter of 1990, many students throughout the U.S. were feeling the same way Joel did. They were forming environmental action groups and writing to their political representatives, demanding laws to save the dolphins.

Some were boycotting the companies who bought tuna that had been captured in drift nets. Thousands of students were refusing to pack tuna fish sandwiches in their lunch boxes. Others protested against tuna in their school cafeterias. One Colorado high school student named Tami Norton organized a boycott that forced her entire school system to remove tuna from lunchroom menus.

But Joel Rubin didn't know about the tuna boycotts that were going on elsewhere. He kept asking himself, what can I do? He called the producers of the TV show, the Earth Island Institute, and asked for more information. When a package arrived, the information made him even angrier: he learned that ten million dolphins had died at the hands of tuna fishers since 1960.

He also learned that the tuna fishers didn't have to use the drift nets; there were nets available that could open to release dolphins trapped inside.

Joel went to Dr. Hackett, his biology teacher, and told him about the show. Dr. Hackett was Joel's favorite teacher, an energetic, fast-talking man who seemed to spill over with ideas. They brainstormed together each day after class. After about two weeks, an idea began to take form. "We came up with the idea of starting a message-writing campaign aimed at a big company that buys tuna from the fishing boats using the drift nets. It started out really loose, but each day we worked out more details."

Joel figured the U.S. companies who bought the tuna were deserving targets. After all, they had the power to refuse to buy tuna caught in drift nets. If they did, the people who caught the fish would have to change their ways or lose business.

Joel decided to try to convince his schoolmates to write hundreds of messages to the H. J. Heinz Company. Joel had always thought of Heinz as a ketchup maker, but he had learned that Heinz also owned the world's biggest tuna company, Star-Kist. At the time, Star-Kist bought some of its tuna from fishers like those in the TV show.

Joel made a presentation to every science class in his school. "I asked their teachers to let me talk to the students. I needed their help. I told them what was going on with the dolphins and the facts I had learned. It was the first time most of them had heard about it. Most were as disgusted as I was."

Joel asked for volunteers to write personal messages to the Heinz Company. "I told them I didn't want anyone who didn't honestly want to work on this to be in on it. It had to be honest. Not a single student turned me down."

GETTING PERSONAL

After talking more with Dr. Hackett, Joel decided the best

strategy would be to send postcards to the homes of the H. J. Heinz Company's executives. Postcards would work better than letters, he thought, since family members would notice them and read the messages. "I imagined the kids of these people showing the cards to their parents when they came home from work and asking, 'What's this?' I thought that would help make the executives think about what they were doing."

And home was more personal than the office. "If we just wrote letters to the company," says Joel, "they would just get thrown in a pile by a secretary. We wanted to have the postcards waiting at home each night after a day at the office."

How many executives should they send cards to? Not just one, since one could just throw all the cards away and no one else in the company would know. Not too many, either, since they wanted a few targeted individuals to feel responsible. Three sounded about right.

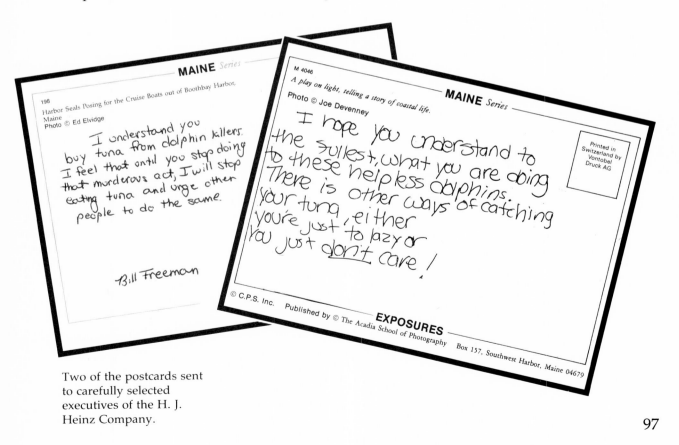

Two of the postcards sent to carefully selected executives of the H. J. Heinz Company.

Next Joel and Dr. Hackett went to the library to try to find out whom to send the cards to. The reference librarian brought out a book called *Standard and Poor's Register of Corporations, Directors and Executives.* It listed the names of the top executives in most of the big companies in America. *Volume Two: Directors and Executives* told a little bit about each boss.

They picked the president of the company, the head of the fish division, and the head of public relations — the person who is responsible for the company's public image.

Now they needed to find home addresses. The company headquarters was in Pittsburgh, so they found a copy of the Pittsburgh telephone directory in the library. They found addresses for three people with the right names, including their middle initials.

Dr. Hackett had a friend who lived in Pittsburgh. The friend called the three houses and asked if there was someone there who worked for the Heinz Company. Bingo.

They bought postcards of Maine, and the next day at school Joel passed them out in the science classes. He asked each student to write three postcards, one to each executive's address, and return them to him. He hadn't decided yet whether to send them all at once or a few each day.

And just to be fair, before he sent them, Joel wrote a letter to Anthony O'Reilly, the president of the Heinz Company asking him to stop buying tuna caught in drift nets. "I explained to him what we were prepared to do and why," Joel says. "I didn't give away the details. I gave him two weeks to reply. He never answered."

Joel decided to mail six cards a day to each of the three executives. He figured that was just about the right amount so that each card would get read. When O'Reilly's deadline passed, Joel took the first six to the mailbox and dropped them in.

Two weeks later, Joel received an angry reply from one of the executives. "He was really upset," Joel says. "He wrote: 'I believe it is inappropriate to be mailing business correspondence to people's homes. I resent this as it crosses the border from professional to personal life. . . . I expect that I will not be hearing from you again.''

Joel took the letter to school and passed it around the science classes. ''We had a little celebration in class that day,'' Joel says, ''because it showed we were getting somewhere. As for getting too personal, we felt very personally about the death of thousands of dolphins. We kept right on mailing to his home.''

About a month later, in April of 1990, Heinz suddenly gave in. Anthony O'Reilly announced at a press conference that Heinz would start buying only tuna that were caught in nets that allowed dolphins to escape. Star-Kist tuna cans would say ''Dolphin Safe'' so that shoppers would know that no dolphins had been killed.

On the same day, two other big tuna companies, Bumble Bee and Van Camp, announced that they would do the same. Together, those three companies bought about seven out of every ten cans of tuna sold in the United States. It was an amazing victory.

In explaining why Star-Kist was making the change, Mr. O'Reilly held up several postcards from high school students in Cape Elizabeth, Maine. One read: ''How can you sleep at night knowing your company is doing this?'' O'Reilly said that even his own children had been urging him to stop killing dolphins.

Joel Rubin was on vacation with his family in California while O'Reilly was speaking. He happened to be at the Earth Island Institute, hoping to get more information, when he heard the news. The staff gathered around to congratulate him for inspiring the powerful postcards. In its own way, the news was almost as shocking as the television show had been a few months before. ''It was an unbelievable feeling to know that I had something to do with helping to solve a big environmental problem,'' he says.

What was it that made the postcard campaign so effective? Joel believes several factors were key:

▲ ▲ ● ■

"I AM IN FAVOR OF ANI-MAL RIGHTS AS WELL AS HUMAN RIGHTS. IT IS THE WAY OF A WHOLE HUMAN BEING."
— ABRAHAM LINCOLN

■ ■ ● ■ ■

● *We believed deeply in what we were doing. It really came from our hearts.*

▲ *We made the campaign personal. We tried to find the people most responsible for the problem and tell them we expected* them *to change it.*

■ *The messages were very simple. Some of the best postcards just said, "Why are you doing this?" or "How can you sleep at night?" They got right to the point.*

● *We weren't scared of a big company. I learned that you don't always have to be polite. The company wasn't polite to dolphins, so why should we beg, "Oh, please, please, would you stop doing that?"*

▲ *We assumed we would succeed. We didn't even think about failing.*

■ *We took chances and were ready to change plans.*

● *We gave our target a chance to do the right thing before we started. We tried to be fair.*

"What happened is amazing," Joel says. "It just goes to show that if you really try, and plan, you can make a difference."

Joel Rubin enjoys a swim with a friend.

CREATING
A
SAFER
FUTURE

FOR US TO CREATE A BETTER LIFE FOR OUR COMMUNITY WE HAVE TO DO IT TOGETHER, WE HAVE TO LOVE AND CARE FOR EACH OTHER. NO ONE PERSON CAN DO IT ALONE.
— FROM THE "PRINCIPLES OF UNITY," WRITTEN BY FREE MY PEOPLE, A POLITICAL ORGANIZATION OF YOUNG ADULTS BASED IN ROXBURY, MASSACHUSETTS

ARN CHORN

▲ ■ ● Arn Chorn of Cambodia was forced to leave his home by an invading army called the Khmer Rouge when he was eight. Soon after, he was separated from his family and forced to work all day in rice paddies with other young children. They had little to eat. Some starved. When Arn was twelve, an army from Vietnam invaded Cambodia and began to fight the Khmer Rouge. Arn was given a gun and forced to become a soldier. A year later, he escaped into the jungle and later became a refugee. He was taken to the United States at fourteen. Though he still has nightmares of war, Arn has used the story of his life to build hope for other children of war. This account begins n the day Arn became a soldier.

One morning when he was twelve and a prisoner of the Khmer Rouge soldiers, Arn Chorn heard the sound of nearby guns. The sky went dark with the smoke of bombs. The soldiers told him the Vietnamese were invading his country, Cambodia.

"The Khmer Rouge quickly rounded up all the kids they could find and gave us guns," Arn recalls. "They said it was up to us to stop the Vietnamese. I didn't care about the Vietnamese. I only wanted to find my mother. But I knew the Khmer Rouge would kill me if I didn't fight."

Arn had never fired a gun. He tried to figure out how to load it. Finally he asked one of his captors, "Where do you put the bullets?" "Figure it out for yourself, stupid," the man said, shoving Arn forward.

Arn's first battle was in a rice paddy. "There were no trees around. No cover. The Vietnamese were very good soldiers. I was terrified when I saw them up close, and I realized how well they could shoot.

102

"I could hear bullets everywhere. The Khmer Rouge had put us children on the front lines, using us as a shield. They were right behind us. If we tried to escape, they would shoot us. If we made a wrong move, the Vietnamese would shoot us. Kids were falling in back of me and in front of me.

"My only thought was to save my life. I kept standing, shooting, falling again, and trying to figure out how to load my gun. Somehow, I survived that first day."

The next day, the Khmer Rouge gave Arn a much heavier gun, an AK-47, which is like a machine gun. "Of course I had never shot one before. The first time I did, it knocked me backward onto the ground. I thought I had been hit. I prayed to God I wouldn't die. I got up and fired the gun again. It knocked me on my butt again. Somehow I survived the second day."

Each day the Vietnamese soldiers pushed Arn's unit deeper and deeper into the jungle. In desperation, the Khmer Rouge changed tactics. "Now they told us to fight as guerrillas," Arn recalls. "Only two or three people were to go out at a time, sneaking through the bushes and trying to surprise the Vietnamese close up. They wanted the smaller ones to go, children like me. They told us to get up as close as we could, until we could hear the Vietnamese talking, and then shoot them and run.

"Sometimes I didn't know whether I was shooting at a Vietnamese or a Cambodian. I just shot. Sometimes these guys would crawl so close to me, I had no choice but to shoot. I had to shoot or be shot. When I killed people, I didn't want to think about what I had done. I would say, 'No, that could not have been my bullet.' "

SNAKES AND MONKEYS

Soon Arn decided he could kill no more. One night, carrying only his hammock and his rifle, Arn slipped alone into the dark jungle. For the next six months, he wandered alone, not knowing where he was, living mainly on fruit that monkeys threw on the ground and fish that he was able to spear with his bayonet. Each night he slung his hammock

▲ ▲ ● ▬▬▬
"IN A WAR YOU HAVE TO FEEL ANGRY ALL THE TIME. ANGER LETS YOU MAKE A DECISION QUICKLY. THERE IS NO TIME FOR CARING. IF YOU CARE, YOU WILL DIE."
— ARN CHORN
▬▬▬ ● ■ ■

103

between tree limbs and crawled in. Sometimes he would wake to feel a snake crawling over his skin. He lay as still as he could until he could fling the snake away.

He was terribly lonely. He wondered where his mother and aunt and beloved sister were. "The saddest and most peaceful times I had in the jungle were with monkeys. I watched the parent monkeys holding their kids. I was so jealous. I wanted somebody to hold me."

One morning, after months beneath the dense leaves, he came to a clearing. Taking a chance, he put down his rifle and wandered, hands up, into what proved to be a refugee camp. He remained there for two years until an American worker named Peter Pond got permission to bring Arn and two other Cambodian boys to the United States. They were the first three children ever to be allowed to go.

"PRONOUNCE IT!"

In 1980, when Arn was fourteen, he found himself living no longer in the jungle but with the Pond family in a big house in New Hampshire. He still had no idea if his Cambodian family was alive. The Ponds had adopted him as a son and tried to make him feel comfortable, but everything was new and strange. Nightmares were still in his head. He didn't feel safe. And he still had some of his old jungle habits.

"Every night I slept on the floor because I couldn't get used to a bed. I couldn't believe that now I had plenty of food and that I no longer had to hunt. At night, I would go to the refrigerator almost every hour and take food back to my room. I would put bananas under my pillow so I could eat them in the night. I wanted to eat them by myself, like I used to. I would finish the banana and put the peel on the floor. When my new mother would come in to wake me in the morning, she would become angry when she saw the banana peels all over the floor."

Even though Arn spoke almost no English, school officials insisted that he enter ninth grade because he was fourteen. He hadn't been to school since he was eight years old.

104

"It was so hard to learn to speak English at first. I tried hard, because there were so many things I wanted to say and ask. My English teacher kept wanting me to say 'th,' but there is no 'th' in Cambodian. She kept going, 'TH: pronounce it!' Finally I got so angry, I spat in her face. I was sent to the principal."

Arn kept trying to learn English, at school and at home. He believed that by telling his own story, he could inspire Americans to try to get other Cambodian children out of the horrible war in Southeast Asia. But first he had to have the words.

Peter Pond suggested that Arn try to give a speech at the church the Ponds attended. Slowly, working until late at night, Peter helped Arn choose words, one after another. It took a whole week for Arn to write, and then memorize, these words: "My name is Arn Chorn. I am a refugee. I am fourteen years old. I came from Cambodia. I have seen many people killed. I have many friends in refugee camps. They are in danger. Please help me. Thank you."

When Sunday came, Arn stood at the pulpit and looked out at the congregation. He said, "My name is Arn Chorn," and then the memory of war swept over him. He began to cry. Steadying himself, he went on. He could see other people crying, too. Somehow, it felt good. When it was over, they formed rows of people to shake his hand. They promised to try to help.

"Right then I began to feel good about myself. I saw that even though I was young, my words could move people. I knew that if I could speak better, I could help my people. I became determined to learn quickly."

CHILDREN OF WAR

In June of 1982, when Arn was sixteen, he was invited to speak as part of a peace rally before a great crowd in the Church of Saint John the Divine in New York City. "I said what living with war had been like for me. Two or three other kids my age spoke, too. One was from Nicaragua, and one was from Japan. Her mother had been killed by the atomic bomb Hiroshima. I had never heard of Hiroshima before that day."

Joining hands with the other children on the stage, Arn concluded his speech with the prayer, "Please may our suffering help other children to grow in peace."

A young woman named Judith Thompson was in the audience. As a college student, she had studied what war was doing to millions of children throughout the world. After graduation she had been working with Cambodian refugees.

A week later, she drove out to the Pond house. At first Arn didn't know what she wanted. "You know those kids who spoke with you at the cathedral?" she said. "They don't know where their parents are either. Why don't we bring together children from around the world to speak to other children about their experiences of war, about their suffering. To show them what we all have in common. Maybe then we could stop fighting. You're a good speaker, Arn. Will you help me raise money to get started?" Arn quickly agreed. Here was a way to use his own experience to bring children together. Trying to raise funds would allow him to practice speaking.

For the next month, Arn told his story to many audiences and asked them to donate money to start a group called Children of War. By the end of 1984, they had raised enough money to assemble forty-five children from sixteen war-torn nations at a house in New Jersey to prepare for the first Children of War tour.

There were children and teens from Cambodia and Vietnam, from Iraq and Iran, from Palestine and Israel, and both a Protestant and a Catholic from Northern Ireland. Their plan was to visit cities throughout the U.S., sharing their stories with American kids to show that it was possible to think beyond war. But first, as traditional enemies, they had to learn to accept each other.

For the next two weeks, the kids practiced being together in peace. First they got into a bus and sat next to those they had been trained to hate most. They made a rule:

"TEACHING A CHILD NOT TO STEP ON A CATERPIL-LAR IS AS VALUABLE TO THE CHILD AS IT IS TO THE CATERPILLAR."
— BRADLEY MILLER

106

they could argue all they wanted, but they couldn't harm each other. Anyone who fought was off the bus.

Arn sat down next to a Vietnamese boy. They avoided looking at each other for a moment — and then began to scream. "You killed my family!" Arn cried. "It's not my fault!" the boy screamed back. "At first I wanted to kill him," Arn recalls, "and surely he wanted to kill me."

The whole bus rang with screams and shouts. And when they got off the bus, they talked all night. Arn's knowledge of the world grew rapidly as he listened to the others tell their stories. Only a few years before, he hadn't even known there was such a place as the United States. And he thought that Cambodians were the only people in the world who killed each other.

At the end of two weeks, each young person stood to share their feelings before the others. Most broke into tears. "We cried and cried. We tried to hug each other for the first

Children of War from around the world overcome their differences and join hands.

time. Some people couldn't. We sang to each other. We had thought that we were different from each other, but we had everything in common. We had lost our families. Our governments had poisoned our minds against each other. We came to see that others had done this to us. We had not done it to each other."

By the time the bus took off to start the tour, they were a family. They spoke to children in twenty-seven cities. They found that most kids they met were caught in the middle of conflicts, too. Many said they were suffering — from shattered families, from loneliness, from being put down because their skin was dark, from feeling that there was little hope or purpose in their lives. Some talked tough and dressed tough to protect themselves. Some were in gangs. Some said they had even considered taking their own lives.

When they were able to talk — kid to kid — about the things that were bothering them, some could see themselves not as losers or victims but as courageous survivors who had done the best they could in tough situations — like the Children of War.

Using their own experiences, the kids on the tour encouraged those they met to find what they had in common — even if it was pain — and to see even those who are supposed to be their enemies as people. They hoped their experiences would inspire young people not to take sides, but to join together to end violence and build hope for the future.

▲ ▲ ● ▬▬▬

"HOW DO YOU KNOW WHETHER A PERSON YOU HAVEN'T MET IS GOOD OR BAD?"

— ARN CHORN

▬▬▬ ● ■ ■

"I HAVE LIVED A HUNDRED LIVES."

Arn Chorn is now a college student. Ever since his first awkward speech in the Ponds' church, he has devoted his life to speaking out against war.

"Everyone asks me, 'What can a kid do?' " Arn says. "There are many things. Form a peace group in your town or school. Join an Amnesty International group. Make a decision. Help poor people. Help people your own age. Speak out. Volunteer. Help inner-city kids. If you have money, save your allowance and give it to people or causes that need it more than you do.

"I have been to thirty countries now. I tell children, children who dream of being a soldier, of being a hero, about my life in war.

"And this is what I tell them: war is horrible. It deadens the heart. Because of war, I have lost much of my family. I still have nightmares. Because of war, I already feel like I have lived a hundred lives."

▲ ▲ ● ▬▬▬

"I HAVE SPOKEN TO MANY CHILDREN WHO WANT TO BE RAMBO. I SAW A MOVIE ONCE WHERE RAMBO TAKES ON PRACTICALLY THE WHOLE VIETNAMESE ARMY BY HIMSELF, AND WINS. I HAD TO LAUGH. I KNOW VIETNAMESE SOLDIERS. RAMBO WOULDN'T HAVE LASTED FIVE MINUTES BY HIMSELF OUT THERE."
— ARN CHORN

▬▬▬ ● ■ ■

Children of War is starting its fourth tour of the United States, this time focusing on inner-city war zones. To contact or support the group, write:

Children of War
85 South Oxford Street
Brooklyn, NY 11217

Arn Chorn.

LINDA WARSAW
AND KIDS AGAINST CRIME

▲ ■ ●

LINDA WARSAW WAS ONLY ELEVEN WHEN SHE FOUNDED KIDS AGAINST CRIME TO TEACH KIDS HOW TO PROTECT THEMSELVES AGAINST CHILD ABUSE. TODAY HER GROUP HAS MORE THAN 4,500 MEMBERS.

One late summer day in 1985, eleven-year-old Linda Warsaw ran up the front walk to her house in San Bernadino, California. A few steps from the door, she froze. The door was open. She and her mother slowly poked their heads in and saw their belongings scattered all over the floor. Linda rushed to her bedroom. Her drawers had been emptied, and her clothes were strewn about the room. Her mattress had been dumped over on the floor. Her tape recorder was gone.

For weeks after the break-in, when Linda and her mother, Nellie, drove home from Linda's school, they sat in the driveway honking the car horn for a while to give any burglars plenty of time to escape.

Finally they decided to do something useful with their fear and anger. They volunteered to work at the San Bernadino County district attorney's office in a special program to help victims of crimes. That, they figured, was one subject they knew about.

The DA's office bustled with lawyers and case workers, cops and witnesses and victims of crimes. Linda's jobs were to open the mail, put postage on letters, make photocopies, and do other office work. She loved all the action around the office. She especially enjoyed talking with the lawyers and case workers about the crimes, about who was guilty and innocent, about what had really happened.

But it could be upsetting, too. Every day Linda heard people talk about children who had been abused by their baby-sitters, relatives, or neighbors. Usually the abusers had warned the children not to tell anyone. Linda worried about her friends. Maybe one of them was being molested, too, she thought. What if they didn't think they could tell anyone? What if they didn't even think they could tell *her*?

Linda began to dream about the cases at night. "I would wake up and think, No, these things can't be happening. No one would really do that stuff to kids. Finally I wanted to see some child abuse hearings for myself. I wanted to know for sure that these weren't just stories."

The DA's office arranged for Linda and her mother to attend five hearings. The last one she saw was the trial of a baby-sitter accused of sexually abusing an eight-year-old girl. Linda squeezed her mother's hand as the baby-sitter's lawyer badgered the young girl, trying hard to confuse her. "What was your baby-sitter wearing?" "What time did it happen?" "How do you know?"

Linda shuddered. Kids shouldn't have to hurt like that girl. They shouldn't have to be victims of whatever adults wanted to do to them. They should be able to fight back. Linda wondered if the girl had any other kid she could talk to. All the people around her were adults. The baby-sitter, the police, the lawyers, the case workers, her parents, the judge — everyone was much older. Could she trust anyone her own age? And even if she could, would a young friend know how to help her?

Linda was silent on the way home, lost in an idea. When she and her mother got home, Linda pulled out a chair at the kitchen table and began to scribble down a long list of thoughts.

The ideas came pouring out onto the paper. She would start a new organization run by kids to help stop crimes against young people. Kids would learn to help each other. They could start a telephone hot line *for* kids to be operated *by* kids. They would organize workshops for kids on crime prevention. Kids would act out ways to prevent crime in skits, and they would invite experts to give training sessions to kids on how to fight child abuse.

Linda sketched out the whole structure of her organization, with chapters in schools, committees of kids, a youth board of directors, and a list of adult advisors. She would be president. Her mom would help. Actually, wasn't that her mom speaking to her at that very moment? Something about dinner. "I can't, Mom," Linda said without looking up, and went on writing.

When Linda finished, it was late and her list was six pages long. "Then I went to bed," Linda remembers. "When I woke up the next morning, there it was, looking at me. All I had to figure out was what to do with it."

KIDS AGAINST CRIME

How, she wondered, do you turn a dream into an organization? She started by typing up her list into a proposal for a group called Kids Against Crime, or KAC. First she stated the group's purpose — to inform young people about how to protect themselves from abuse. Then she listed the group's activities and proposed things like how often they would meet and how they would learn enough about child abuse to help other children.

Then Linda began showing the proposal to her friends and classmates, to workers at the DA's office, to the police chief, to people who worked with crime and children. She asked for their ideas and added the best of them to her proposal. Many volunteered to help before she even asked.

On a Wednesday evening in May, Linda and eighteen other young people gathered with Nellie in a small room at the DA's office. The DA had offered to let them use the room as their headquarters and gave them the use of a typewriter and a photocopy machine.

They divided up into research committees so they could learn about different kinds of crimes. They wanted to know why such crimes happened, who was most likely to commit them, what the early warning signs might be. Each committee had to present a report at the next meeting.

The next week, forty kids jammed into the DA's office. Linda chose eleven who seemed most interested — she wanted an odd number to break tie votes — to be the first members of KAC's youth board of directors. After that, there would be elections. The board would come up with ideas for Kids Against Crime.

A police officer showed them how to fingerprint each other and fill out identification records. KAC's idea was to fingerprint as many kids as possible and give the prints to their families. Then if kids turned up missing, the families would be able to provide something that would help detectives search for them.

The next month, the San Bernadino police department invited KAC to set up a fingerprinting booth at a local mall. Hundreds of curious children dragged their parents to the KAC booth. Most of them signed up to become KAC members. The following Wednesday, over a hundred kids tried to wedge into the DA's office for a KAC meeting.

Soon they had outgrown the DA's office. For a while they met at the public library, but even that became too small. Linda decided to ask the mayor for help. "Linda was amazing," her mother says. "She would ask anybody for anything. She would just call someone like the mayor up and say, 'I have a program and I need your support.' The mayor would say, 'Come over,' and soon I would find myself driving her to a meeting."

The mayor found them a free office, and a furniture store owner donated a roomful of desks, tables, and chairs. Linda invited crime experts to become members of KAC's adult advisory board. Linda explained to each expert that young people were running the group but that she needed their knowledge to help make the kids' programs work. Soon the mayor, the district attorney, the chief of police, and several social workers had said yes.

Linda Warsaw calls a meeting of Kids Against Crime to order.

KAC, Inc.

By 1987, they were growing way too fast. So many KAC chapters were opening in schools throughout San Bernadino that it was soon too expensive to even print their newsletter and send out notices of meetings. They had been operating without dues, asking each family to chip in a little for expenses and refreshments. Now the cost of stamps alone was breaking them. "It had never occurred to me," Linda recalls, "that organizations run on money."

They began to add professional fund-raisers to the adult board, as well as lawyers and media executives, people who could help them control the growth of their organization before it ate them alive. A turning point came when a lawyer offered to help Kids Against Crime become a nonprofit corporation. That way, he explained, anyone — and that meant individuals, companies, and private foundations — who gave KAC money wouldn't have to pay taxes on their gift. Then they could try to get big grants, even grants from the government. Basically, he said, KAC would become a business, but they could only use the money they raised to pay for the expenses and activities of the organization.

Kids Against Crime clean up graffiti in Los Angeles.

In their first two years since they became a nonprofit corporation, KAC has raised nearly $100,000 from companies, foundations, clubs, a union, and the City of San Bernadino. Now KAC has more than 4,500 members in forty-five states and five countries, a small paid staff, and offices in three cities. Some of KAC's activities include:

▲ A toll-free hot line that lets kids with problems talk to other kids who have been trained to listen and help. "If they have a problem, our operators can refer them to professionals who can help them," says Linda. In order to work on the hot line, young people must be between the ages of twelve and nineteen and have to attend at least twenty-four hours of training workshops.

■ Workshops dealing with crimes against children. "Kids wrote skits, acting out how to recognize when something is wrong and what to do about it," says Linda. "We put together a skit booklet that other kids could use."

● Fingerprinting. To date, KAC has fingerprinted over 20,000 children.

▲ Grafitti cleanups. "We sponsor events so that the whole city — kids, parents, businesses, cops — get together to scrub graffiti."

"WITH HELP, YOU CAN DO ANYTHING."

Now Linda is nineteen and in her second year of college, but often she can still be found at KAC headquarters in San Bernadino. Usually she is in a small booth, her ear pressed tightly against one of the three red hot line phones, listening intently to young people who call about everything from loneliness to drugs to danger in their lives. She listens to their stories and talks to them patiently. Sometimes she is able to refer them to someone who can help, sometimes not. But always she provides support just by being there.

On many nights, Linda is seated beside a fifteen-year-old girl who takes calls in the next booth. She was abandoned by her parents and adopted by her grandparents, who then

Kids Against Crime uses this logo to help convey their message.

mistreated her and abandoned her, too. Since then she has lived in a series of foster homes, none of which has been a happy place. A year ago, she was thinking a lot about dying. She believed no one wanted her and that she had nothing to give.

She found out about KAC at a fingerprinting booth and joined a chapter. Now instead of being told she is worthless, she can use her experience to help kids who call the hot line. She says it gives her a feeling of satisfaction and meaning in her life to think she can help someone else avoid harm.

Linda knows that because of KAC, kids like the eight-year-old girl she saw at the trial years ago have a better chance of surviving abuse. They have other kids to talk to, kids who won't judge them, kids who can keep secrets, kids with information, kids who know where to get help.

"I think anyone who really wants to help others can make a difference," Linda says. "Even when you're very young, as I was. You can succeed if you build support from others — friends, teachers, parents like my mom, anyone. With some help, I really believe you can do anything."

Linda Warsaw.

To become a member of KAC, contact them at:

Kids Against Crime
P.O. Box 22004
San Bernadino, CA 92406

KAC's hot line number is 1-800-522-5670. The line is open from 3:00 to 9:00 P.M. (Pacific time) on weekdays and twenty-four hours a day on weekends.

116

THE CHILDREN'S STATUE FOR PEACE

▲■■● **INSPIRED BY THE STORY OF SADAKO SASAKI, A JAPANESE GIRL WHO DIED AFTER AN ATOM BOMB EXPLODED OVER HER CITY AT THE END OF WORLD WAR II, FIFTEEN THIRD- AND FOURTH-GRADERS IN NEW MEXICO SET OUT TO BUILD A STATUE TO REMIND THE WORLD THAT CHILDREN WANT AND DESERVE A FUTURE FREE OF NUCLEAR WEAPONS. THREE YEARS LATER, THOUSANDS OF KIDS HAVE JOINED THE PROJECT. THEY PLAN TO BUILD IT IN THE VERY PLACE WHERE THE BOMB THAT KILLED SADAKO WAS MADE.**

The Children's Statue for Peace started with a single word. In February of 1990, a teacher named Carrie Gassner in Albuquerque, New Mexico, wrote the word *War* on the blackboard. That, they all agreed, was the problem. It was up to the third- and fourth-grade students in the class she cotaught with Christine Luke to propose solutions.

When they were finished, the one they liked best was "Work on peace." The question then became "How?" And when they were done talking about it, two ideas were left on the blackboard. One was "Start a fund for peace," and the other was "March for peace."

The class decided to combine the two. The next day the children sold popcorn at lunch, raising $11.90. The following week, on a blustery Valentine's Day, fifteen children proudly marched to the neighborhood bank to deposit the money and start the peace fund.

Dana Kaplan, who was in Ms. Gassner's class, remembers how it felt. "About fifteen kids walked in carrying a big banner that said, 'Peace.' Then we sang to the tellers, songs

▲ ▲ ● ■ ■

"WAR IS AN INVENTION OF THE HUMAN MIND. THE HUMAN MIND CAN INVENT PEACE WITH JUSTICE."
—NORMAN COUSINS

■ ■ ● ■ ■

117

like 'One Tin Soldier.' We passed out valentines to the customers. The people in the bank were giving us the weirdest looks, like, 'Why are they doing this?' "

The next week, Ms. Luke invited a puppeteer named Camy Condon to give a performance focused on the theme of world peace. When she was finished, Camy told them the story of Sadako Sasaki, a girl who lived in Hiroshima, Japan, when an atomic bomb was dropped on her city at the end of World War II.

Sadako became ill with radiation sickness. It is a Japanese tradition that anyone who folds one thousand paper cranes will have their deepest wish come true. From her hospital bed, Sadako set out to fold one thousand paper cranes. When she died, she had folded 644 cranes. Just before she died, she held up one of them and said, "I will write peace on your wings, and you will fly all over the world." Her classmates folded the remaining 356 cranes and raised money to build a beautiful peace statue of Sadako, which now stands in Hiroshima. Each year, children from all over the world visit the statue.

When Camy was finished, she showed them a string of one thousand paper cranes that she had brought back from a visit to Japan. It took several students to help her hold them up. They were of all colors. It was then they had their idea. "Let's build a peace statue here," one of the children said. Impulsively, the puppeteer said, "I'll help you."

THE KIDS' COMMITTEE

As a first step, they formed the Kids' Committee to Build a Peace Statue, with Camy and the two teachers as adult advisers. They chose as their headquarters Pistol Pete's Pizza, a loud, bright room well known to almost all children in Albuquerque. They placed an ad in the Albuquerque Peace Center's newsletter. It read: "Kids' Committee meeting. Everyone welcome. Last Sunday of the month. 1:00. Pistol Pete's."

Forty kids showed up. The owner offered to give Kids' Committee members a dollar off each pizza if they would make Pete's their official headquarters. So on the last Sunday of each month, young activists, mouths full of pepperoni and anchovies, began to fashion an international symbol for peace.

First they decided to hold a press conference to introduce the project to people around Albuquerque and to attract more kids. They set a date in April and wrote to schools and church youth groups throughout New Mexico. Bonnie Malcolm, a tall high school sophomore with a slow, level way of talking, called reporters and invited them to come.

A press conference brings attention to the Children's Peace Statue.

On a bright April Saturday morning, twelve Kids' Committee members sat at a row of card tables, blinking into the desert sun at a group of reporters. They had tacked up a row of posters behind them as a backdrop for photographers.

They all gave statements. Then one reporter called out, "Where are you going to build the statue?" "Los Alamos," Bonnie blurted out. Everyone looked at her. No one had ever discussed it. "It's the perfect connection," she explained, smiling. The bomb that ended up destroying Hiroshima had been built in Los Alamos, a town about a hundred miles north of where they stood. There was a children's statue for peace in Hiroshima. Why not one in Los Alamos?

▲ ▲ ● ■■■■

"THROUGH THIS PROJECT WE WILL SAY TO EVERYONE THAT PEACE IS NECESSARY AND THAT WARS ARE NOT. WHOEVER SAID THAT CHILDREN SHOULD BE SEEN AND NOT HEARD WAS STUPID. NOW THEY'LL HEAR US."

— BONNIE MALCOLM

■■■■ ● ■ ■

119

Then it was time for their most dramatic idea. Two kids hoisted up the nose cone of an old missile that Camy had bought for four dollars at an army surplus sale. They turned it upside down and carried it through the audience, asking people to drop in donations for the statue. When they were finished, there was $102 in the missile's point. They took out the money and then carried the cone to a corner of the school playground, where they scooped handfuls of earth into its hollow end. They then planted bright yellow marigolds in it and jammed the point into a hole in the ground, tamping the earth in around it. Before everyone's eyes — and cameras — a weapon had turned into a planter.

The Kids' Committee finds a new use for the nose cone of a missile.

120

The next morning, the *Albuquerque Journal* printed a big story about their project and even an editorial supporting them. Part of the editorial read:

These students, ages 5 to 17, are learning, organizing, planning, assuming responsibility, working toward a goal and making commitments. Keep it up, keep it growing and this world will more likely see further generations of peace.

It was amazing: only three months after Ms. Gassner had written *War* on the blackboard, they had an idea, a growing team, a headquarters, and a place they wanted the statue to be. Back at Pete's, they laid out a simple five-year plan:

▲ 1990: Tell other kids in New Mexico.
■ 1991: Tell kids in all fifty states. Reach out to the world.
● 1992: Collect models and designs for the statue.
▲ 1993: Select a site and make a model of the statue.
■ 1994: Begin to build the statue.
● 1995: Dedicate the statue in a ceremony on August 6, the fiftieth anniversary of the bombing of Hiroshima.

Caitlin Chestnut, who volunteered to be the editor of *The Crane*, shows the first issue.

Kids began working hard to raise money for the project. Everyone tried their own ideas. Two hundred dollars came in from a candy sale at a school. There were bake sales and silver dollar sales. A church walk-a-thon raised $1,744. They wrote to a foundation and got $500. A local artist designed a T-shirt free, and soon they were selling shirts with the picture of a crane surrounded by the words *Kids' Committee Children's Peace Statue.*

The New Mexico Council of Churches, a tax-exempt organization, agreed to act as a sponsor for the project so that anyone who donated money would not have to pay taxes on their gift.

Leaders emerged one by one. Dana Kaplan volunteered to keep track of T-shirt orders. Caitlin Chestnut, then in seventh grade, volunteered to edit a newsletter for the project, which they decided to call *The Crane*.

121

At one meeting, the Kids' Committee decided to try to gather one million signatures of children on a peace petition and to try to raise a dollar from every child who signed. Someone pointed out that for a million letters, they would need a post office box. Veronica Roe picked out a box that was on the bottom row of boxes at the post office so that even small children could put the key in and open the box.

Kids' Committee members fanned out on weekends and evenings and spoke in bookstores, on radio and TV shows, and in schools and churches, trying to attract new members.

Soon letters with dollars were pouring into P.O. Box 12888.

The project seemed like an organism that begins as a single cell and keeps dividing. As Dana Kaplan puts it, "Unexpected things kept happening." New tasks appeared all the time. Someone had to thank all the people who sent money. Camille Green volunteered and designed lovely cards. Someone had to deposit the money and calculate interest. Students in Ms. Luke and Ms. Gassner's class took it on as a math project.

Most urgent of all, they had to find a better way to keep track of all the kids who were joining. A year after their first meeting, they had heard from over three thousand people, most of whom had sent money, some from as far away as Japan and the Soviet Union. Word was spreading like wildfire. Once again, Bonnie Malcolm took charge. She scooped up a pile of pizza-stained notebooks full of handwritten names and headed home to enter them all on her computer at home. "I think I have a program that will work," she said.

In the spring of 1991, an architect who was a friend of Camy said the Albuquerque chapter of the American Institute of Architects was interested in adopting the peace statue as a project. Their group has over 150 chapters across the United States, with at least one chapter in every state. Was there a way they could help the kids design the statue?

The Kids' Committee turned the offer into a contest.

Children in every state would design peace statues, parks, or monuments. The architects in each state would help select two final designs and would work with the winning children to build small-scale models. Then the one hundred scale models would be sent to New Mexico and shown to children around the state in a traveling exhibition. Finally, the children would choose the winning design, and architects would build it in 1994, using money that the children had raised. It would be ready by August of 1995, in time to draw the world's attention to the bombing of Hiroshima and to their commitment to peace. That sounded good, the architect said. But where exactly will your statue be? That, they told him, was still the big question.

Announcing a contest for the best design of a Children's Statue for Peace.

"PLEASE GIVE US LAND!"

On Tuesday, November 19, 1991, a convoy of buses and cars from nine different schools, carrying 130 children, crawled up the narrow mountain road from Santa Fe to Los Alamos. It is the same road, now paved, that scientists and military officers traveled by mule and Jeep in 1942, looking for a secret place to build the atomic bomb.

The children sang peace songs as the buses and cars bounced past electronic guard stations and into a glass and steel complex of weapons labs.

They were on their way to the Los Alamos library to hold a press conference introducing the statue project to the people of Los Alamos and asking the county government for free land to use for the peace statue.

They knew not everyone in Los Alamos would welcome their project. Many people who worked on the first two atomic bombs still live there. Most of them believe their work saved lives by bringing World War II to a sudden end. A half century later, weaponry has become a huge business in New Mexico, providing thousands of jobs, many in Los Alamos. A statue for peace inspired by a girl who died at Hiroshima would be hard for some to accept.

Carrying signs and banners, the kids poured into the small library. Soon there were so many people in the room

▲ ▲ ● ▬▬▬
"SOMEDAY THEY WILL GIVE A WAR AND NO-BODY WILL COME."
— POET CARL SANDBURG, "THE PEOPLE, YES!"
▬▬▬ ● ■ ■

that some had to stand on stepladders against the back walls. Fourth- and fifth-graders from the John Baker School in Albuquerque carried in a ten-foot-long strand of one thousand paper cranes they had folded and gave it to an amazed librarian.

The children sang and chanted and made speeches. When a man named James Flynt, in charge of land for Los Alamos County, was introduced to them, the children erupted into a chant of "Please give us land!"

Flynt smiled and said only, "I support this project. I will help you." Time will tell just what he meant.

▲ ■ ● "THEN [THE MUSHROOM CLOUD] WAS WASHED OUT WITH THE WIND. WE TURNED TO EACH OTHER AND OFFERED CONGRATULATIONS FOR THE FIRST FEW MINUTES. THEN, THERE WAS A CHILL, WHICH WAS NOT FOR THE MORNING COLD; IT WAS A CHILL THAT CAME TO ONE WHEN ONE THOUGHT, AS FOR INSTANCE WHEN I THOUGHT OF MY WOODEN HOUSE IN CAMBRIDGE, AND MY LABORATORY IN NEW YORK, AND OF THE MILLIONS OF PEOPLE LIVING AROUND THERE."
— PHYSICIST ISIDORE RABI, REMEMBERING HOW HE FELT WHEN HE AND OTHER SCIENTISTS WATCHED THE FIRST ATOMIC BOMB EXPLOSION

"WE CAN REALLY PULL THIS OFF."

Even with all the excitement, sometimes people get discouraged and tired. The Kids' Committee needs more dedicated workers. Some key people have moved away, and a few are doing too much. "Sometimes I feel like saying, 'I don't want any responsibility for a while,'" Caitlin Chestnut says. "And then a check will come in or there will be a great letter to *The Crane*, and I'll get excited again."

Sometimes the project doesn't seem real, especially compared to school projects. There is nothing official about it. It's not for a grade. It seems to grow on its own, and the schedule is whatever the kids decide. They don't know yet what the statue will look like or even where it will be. If they don't do their job, no one will punish them. It just means someone else has to do it.

124

But some see the chance to build a symbol of peace for all children as maybe the best, most real thing they'll ever do. "I plan to stay around till 1995 no matter what," Bonnie Malcolm says firmly. "I won't move away, even for college."

Each Friday afternoon, Bonnie walks to the post office, opens box 12888, and returns to her computer with a bundle of letters.

As the opener of the mail, Bonnie finds unexpected treasures, messages that cause her to shake the fatigue away and keep tapping more names into her "Statue" file.

"Once I opened the post office box," she says, "and found a letter from Japan. It was from a man in Hiroshima. He had been there that day, like Sadako. He's still alive. It began, 'Dear good and brave children: I'm very thankful that all of you, so young and brave, are planning the statue.' I almost couldn't go on reading, it made me so proud. It made me think this is really going to happen. It isn't a dream. We can really pull this off."

The Children's Peace Statue needs designs, volunteers, and signatures. To help, write:

The Children's Peace Statue
New Mexico Council of Churches
P.O. Box 12888
Albuquerque, NM 87195-2888

I will write peace
on your wings
and you will fly all
over the world

-Sadako Sasaki

Sadako Sasaki urged peace despite her suffering after the atom bomb was dropped on Hiroshima.

PART TWO

HOW THEY'RE DOING IT

A Handbook for Young Activists

SECTION **1**

WHY GET INVOLVED?

Here are four reasons:

Why let someone else make your decisions for you?
The students of Lexington High School in Massachusetts
wrote their own constitution for their school. It starts like
this:

> *All members of the school community should have a voice
> in determining the policies of the school, in promoting a
> positive social climate, and in shaping the future of the
> school.*

It took them months to get the school administrators
and teachers to share power. They had to negotiate, and
they didn't get everything they wanted. But now the school
belongs to them, too. Before then, every rule, from the
cafeteria menu to the rules about smoking to what books
they read, were made by adults. As student organizer Alex
Reinert puts it, "I have never understood why a school
board composed entirely of adults would know what's better
for a school than the students themselves."

**One person can make a huge difference in a local com-
munity.** Sarah Rosen fought sexism by trying to change her
school. John DeMarco risked his safety and happiness to
keep *one block* of Philadelphia free from racial discrimination.
Andrew Holleman helped save three endangered species by
preserving their habitats in the forest next door.

Did these people save the world? No, they changed
what they could. And if enough people change what they
can, we can build a better future.

"THIS IS THE TRUE JOY
IN LIFE: BEING USED FOR
A PURPOSE RECOGNIZED
BY YOURSELF AS A
MIGHTY ONE, AND BEING
A FORCE OF NATURE IN-
STEAD OF A FEVERISH,
SELFISH LITTLE CLOD OF
AILMENTS AND GRIEV-
ANCES, COMPLAINING
THAT THE WORLD WILL
NOT DEVOTE ITSELF TO
MAKING YOU HAPPY."
— GEORGE BERNARD SHAW

128

A mission gives you energy. When you are trying to help someone else, or change something that you truly believe is wrong, you feel fully alive. It's exciting. "Being a part of the peace statue project is more satisfying than spending my time at the mall or watching TV," says Dana Kaplan. "I have a lot of responsibility. I'm learning how to deal with money, how to raise funds, how to put my ideas across. It makes me think."

What do you have better to do? You only have so much time to live. You don't know how long that will be. What do you want to do with it? You have the chance to lend your years, your energy, your brief moment, to making this a better place. "My future is now," says peace activist Bonnie Malcolm. "I'm living my life to the fullest right now. It all counts."

HOW TO GET STARTED   SECTION 2

CHOOSE A PROJECT YOU REALLY CARE ABOUT

It doesn't have to be a global issue. In fact, maybe you can help others by doing what you already like to do anyway. Suppose you:

▲ *Love plants* . . . . *Volunteer at a community garden*
■ *Love animals* . . . . *Help an environmental group*
● *Like to build* . . . . *Help build a house for poor people*
▲ *Love to read* . . . . *Tutor someone else*
■ *Play guitar* . . . . *Sing at a senior citizens' center*
● *Like to cook* . . . . *Prepare meals for a shelter*
▲ *Love basketball* . . . . *Organize a benefit game*
■ *Collect things for fun* . . . . *Collect food or clothing for others*
● *Like to draw* . . . . *Put on an art show, and donate the proceeds*

As Justin Lebo puts it:

I didn't know how to build a house for the homeless, and I didn't know how to do a lot of other stuff. But then I realized I knew how to fix bikes. I wanted to help people. So I did that. I could be happy and make other people happy at the same time.

FIND OTHERS TO WORK WITH

As one person, you can make a big difference, but you can usually do more, and have more fun, if you work with others. Look for help in school, in the neighborhood, or through community organizations.

Working with others isn't always easy. Members of even the tightest groups sometimes get jealous, blame each other for failures, accuse each other of not working hard enough, get burned out, or lose interest. Leaders quit. Goals go unmet. Here are a few ways to ward off these problems:

Try to give everyone a definite job. For example, in the Children's Peace Statue project, Bonnie Malcolm keeps track of members on her computer, Caitlin Chestnut edits the newsletter, Dana Kaplan handles T-shirt orders, Camille Green sends thank-you notes, and students in Ms. Gassner's class do financial accounting. Other kids talk to the press, organize events, and answer the mail. Change jobs from time to time so everybody learns to do several things and no one gets stuck in any one job. If you break work into committees, let people work on the committees that interest them the most.

Meet regularly, at the same time and place.

Try to make it fun. Have something to eat. Sing together. Take a break together to do something you like to do.

If there are conflicts, set aside time to talk about them. Try to think of solutions in terms of your vision. Ask yourselves what outcome will best help you all accomplish your goals.

WRITE A VISION STATEMENT

Before you plunge into a project, think about exactly what you want to have accomplished at the end. Brainstorm the idea with others. Dream. Then write a simple statement of your basic vision and a few specific goals. State it positively. Instead of "Stop the development," for example, say "Preserve the marsh."

Keep a copy of your vision statement where you can look at it whenever you need to. When times get tough and you feel lost or doubtful, you can look at the words you wrote at the very beginning and say, "Oh, yeah, I remember. *This* is what we wanted to do."

DON'T LET ADULTS TAKE OVER

Adults have experience, access to power, and sometimes money, equipment, and other resources. Sometimes an adult adviser can help focus a group. But how do you keep adults from taking over?

Write up a charter, which defines your group's purposes and principles. State clearly that it is to be a youth-led group, and specify the roles you want adults to play.

Shop around. Pick only adult advisers you feel comfortable around and really want to work with. Insist that they be committed to the group's goals as you have written them. Tell them exactly how you want them to help: you need fund-raising advice, you need a sponsor for a bill, you need a teacher who will sponsor your group at school. Direct them. Make the driving ideas behind your group be your own.

RESEARCH BEFORE YOU PLUNGE

Find out the following: What is the problem, really? How bad is it? Where does it come from? Who is responsible for controlling it? Why do they let it go on that way? What laws or rules regulate it? Who loses if it gets solved your way? Break up into committees and do some research. With facts, you can design solutions. Without facts, you won't be taken seriously. Here are some research ideas:

▲ ▲ ● ■

"THE IDEA OF YOUNG PEOPLE THINKING FOR THEMSELVES IS THREATENING TO SOME ADMINISTRATORS AND TEACHERS. IF YOU USE AN ADULT ADVISER, YOU NEED SOMEONE COMMITTED TO STUDENTS TAKING A STAND AND ACTING AS LEADERS IN THE SCHOOL. DON'T JUST PICK A TEACHER WHO'S YOUR FRIEND. FIND A STRONG FACULTY MEMBER WHO'S COMMITTED TO YOUR GOALS."
— ALEX REINERT, STUDENT ORGANIZER, BOSTON

■ ■ ● ■ ■

Use the public library. What a great resource a library is! If you need a map, a copy of your town's master plan, lists of places where you could volunteer, ideas for where to get money, the state's laws for water pollution, the names of the leaders of the company whose product you plan to boycott, or a directory of government agencies, go to the library and ask a reference librarian to show you how to look them up.

Good reference librarians love to help people who really want to know things. Tell them about your project. Let them see your excitement. They'll help you smoke out the facts.

Use the telephone book. If information were food, you'd never starve if you had a phone book. Have you ever really checked out your phone book? In it, you can usually find:

▲ A map of every town in the book's area

■ The addresses and phone numbers of every school around

● A map of all the congressional districts in your state

▲ The addresses and phone numbers of your U.S. senators and representatives and your state legislators

■ Phone numbers for the agencies that are supposed to enforce the laws of your state, including the environmental laws

● The area codes and time zones for every part of the U.S.

▲ The zip code of every town in your state

Use the people who represent you at your state capital and in Washington, D.C. They are supposed to work for you. And they will if you make them. U.S. senators and congresspeople hire staff people to help residents of their state or district deal with problems. You also have a state representative and state senators. Call your federal or state legislators on behalf of your group and ask for help. The numbers will be in your phone book.

132

DEVELOP YOUR OWN INFORMATION

Sometimes the best information is the information you find on your own. You can:

Gather statistics. Suppose you're trying to clean up a polluted stream. *List* the junk you see. Take pictures of it. Get your science teacher to show you how to sample the water for pollutants. Get the facts. When Kristin Nunnery and Anna Brown of Freeport, Maine, decided to lobby their town council to stop using polystyrene packages, they first walked half the length of Main Street carrying a plastic bag. They picked up, sorted, and classified every piece of trash they saw. About half of the 165 pieces they collected were made of polystyrenes. When they went to face their town councillors, they were armed with facts that helped persuade the town to pass an ordinance prohibiting the town council from buying polystyrene packaging.

Interview people. A person's firsthand story often gives you the truth behind the statistics. For example, when the schoolchildren of Holmes County, Mississippi, wanted to understand how black citizens in their county won the right to vote, they clicked on tape recorders and interviewed the older people around where they lived. Suddenly they saw their grandparents as important historical figures — which many of them were.

Research both sides of an issue. Understanding where other people are coming from doesn't weaken your case. It gives you a chance to develop arguments that you may need to win. It helps you understand the issues more completely. It lets you design solutions in which everyone can win something.

CREATE A WORK PLAN

Once you have a project, a team, a vision, and some facts, make a plan of action. Start by planning what you're going to do for the first three months. Set goals, list the necessary jobs, assign them, and set deadlines for their completion. Your plan might look like this:

TIPS FOR INTERVIEWING PEOPLE

● THINK CAREFULLY ABOUT WHOM YOU WANT TO INTERVIEW AND WHY HE OR SHE IS IMPORTANT.

■ CALL IN ADVANCE, STATE YOUR PURPOSE, AND ARRANGE AN APPOINTMENT.

▲ WRITE OUT INTERVIEW QUESTIONS.

● KNOW YOUR FIRST QUESTION IN ADVANCE. MAKE IT A GOOD ONE.

■ AVOID YES/NO QUESTIONS. ASK QUESTIONS THAT CAUSE PEOPLE TO ELABORATE.

▲ DON'T SKIP AROUND. ASK ALL THE QUESTIONS YOU WANT IN ONE SUBJECT AREA BEFORE MOVING ON.

● TRY NOT TO INTERRUPT.

■ REHEARSE!

▲ IF YOU USE A TAPE RECORDER, MAKE SURE IT WORKS, THAT YOU HAVE FRESH BATTERIES, AND THAT THE MICROPHONE IS GOOD. DO A SOUND CHECK.

● TRANSCRIBE THE INTERVIEW SOON AFTER YOU FINISH IT.

133

Cole Middle School Art Sale for the Sixth Street Shelter

3-Month Work Plan	Jan 6	13	20	27	Feb 3	10	17	24	Mar 3	10	17	24	31
Write Proposal	SH, PH												
Get Principal's Permission		SH, PH											
Find Teacher to Sponsor Sale	LA, VA												
Present Idea to all Classrooms			SH, TD										
Contact Shelter			RA, LT										
Get Volunteers to Work at Sale				LN, RN									
Arrange Refreshments					SH, VA								
Find Tables					RC								
Set Up Receipt System								HH, RH					
Write Press Release							SH, TD						
Hang Drawings										EVERYONE			
Get Cash, Change												PH	
Sale!												ALL	

TEN TOOLS FOR CHANGE

WRITE A LETTER

The price of a stamp can buy a lot of muscle. You can write a letter to request information, arrange an interview, or tell people what you think. You can ask for support, complain, try for money, or thank those who have helped you.

Here are some tips for letter writers:

▲ Put the date at the top.

■ Be personal. Say who you are and why you care.

● Get right to the point and say what you want.

▲ You don't have to type your letter, but make it neat.

■ Don't try to sound like an adult. Just be yourself.

● Address it to the right person. Often that's the *local* person who has the power to do what you need done. If you want to get rid of graffiti on your school, start with the school board officials rather than your U.S. senators.

▲ Use details. If you have statistics or if you can describe the problem in detail, do so.

■ Say exactly what you want the person to do.

● Keep a copy of your letter. Put it in a file and label the file so you can find it when you need it.

▲ Just close the letter with "Sincerely" and sign your name.

■ Print your name and address on the letter, so the person you are writing to can reply.

▲ ▲ ● ▬▬▬

"IT'S HARD TO BELIEVE HOW LUCKY I'VE BEEN AND HOW MUCH MY LIFE HAS CHANGED BY WRITING THAT LETTER."
— SAMANTHA SMITH

▬▬▬ ● ■ ■

135

Here are some tips for pumping up your letters and turning them into "power letters":

Send copies of your letter to people your targets respect — and tell them you're doing it. Say you want to get a store to quit stocking food items that are overpackaged. If you write a letter to the manager of the store requesting the change, there's a good chance the manager will either ignore it or send back a cheerful letter that doesn't deal with your issue.

But if you send copies of your letter to the president of the company — at home — to your state representative and to the Better Business Bureau — and *say so* on your letter to the manager — he or she almost has to take you seriously. On the opposite page is an example.

Write a letter to your newspaper. Keep it brief and address it to the editor. Sign the names and ages of several in your group. The newspaper may very well print it. The letter then makes a public record of your position and gives you the chance to educate a lot of readers about the issue through just one letter.

Organize a letter-writing campaign. A national letter-writing campaign organized by Kids Against Pollution of Closter, New Jersey, caused McDonald's to switch from foam containers to paper-based wrappings. Research shows that just twenty letters to a representative about the same issue can be enough to make the issue a priority. Make sure each letter is different enough so that the representative doesn't assume they were all written by the same person.

Get to the point, and send copies to your target's bosses and others who could pressure him or her.

[Date]
John F. Kennedy Middle School
Manchester, NH 03301

Ms. Loretta Lettuceleaf, Manager
Super Shop 'n' Spend
11 Monotony Drive
Manchester, NH 03301

Dear Ms. Lettuceleaf:

We are seventh-graders from the John F. Kennedy Middle School. We are writing to urge Shop 'n' Spend not to sell items that contain too much packaging.

Last Wednesday, we took a field trip to your store at the East Doldrum Mall. We counted seventy-two items that had at least four layers of packaging. We have attached a list of those products.

Some packages had hardly any food in them. Take Park Avenue cookies, for example. After you unwrap the outside plastic package, you find a cardboard box. Then there's a plastic tray with three rows inside. Each row is wrapped in plastic. There are only three cookies in each row.

What a waste! $2.59 for nine cookies and a bunch of paper and plastic. Most of this packaging winds up in our landfills, taking up space that we need. Some of it can't be recycled. We want you not to sell overpackaged products. That's the best way to send a message to manufacturers.

We want to meet with you to discuss how Shop 'n' Spend plans to solve this problem. You should know that if we're not satisfied, we plan to organize to put pressure on your store. We'll call soon for an appointment.

Sincerely,

[Names of 21 students]

cc: Mr. Charles Chainowner, President, Super Shop 'n' Spend Co.,
     7190 Comfort Court, Manchester, NH 03301

     Manchester Better Business Bureau

     Ms. Paula Powerbroker, Chairperson, Manchester City Council

USE A PETITION TO BUILD SUPPORT

A petition is a statement of your position that is signed by people who agree with what you want. All those signatures make a petition harder to ignore than a letter.

A petition can:

▲ Give you a chance to educate potential supporters.
■ Give you the names and addresses of people who might stay involved in your effort.
● Give you something that will help attract the attention of decision makers and reporters.

Here are some tips for creating effective petitions:

▲ Give your petition a title that sums up the issue in a few words.
■ Make a copy and file it somewhere so you can find it easily. Don't give your only copy away.
● Make sure the petition asks the people who sign it to give their names, addresses, and telephone numbers, too. That way you know how to reach them if you need their support later.
▲ Call reporters when you deliver the petition to the decision maker.

▲ ▲ ● ▬▬▬▬

"WHEN YOU'RE TRYING TO GET PEOPLE TO SIGN A PETITION, TAKE YOUR TIME. BE PATIENT AND EXPLAIN, EVEN IF YOU HAVE TO SAY THE SAME THING OVER AND OVER. THE MORE PEOPLE KNOW, THE MORE THEY WILL BE WILLING TO HELP YOU."
— ANDREW HOLLEMAN

▬▬▬▬ ● ■ ■

On the opposite page is an example.

In some places, you can force a hearing or even a vote on an issue by starting a legal petition, that is, a petition among registered voters. If enough voters sign, the issue has to be discussed in an official meeting or voted on in a referendum. The rules differ from state to state and even from town to town, so you'll have to check. The secretary of state's office is a good place to start.

Even if you can't vote, it might pay to try to get voters to sign a petition. You can give copies of the petition to politicians to show your issue concerns voters, too. Most important of all, a petition gives you a chance to meet and educate potential supporters.

Here is a petition with a title and a brief, specific description of a problem.

PETITION FOR A TRAFFIC LIGHT AT SIXTH AND MAIN STREETS

We, the students of Tubman Middle School, think there should be a traffic light at the intersection of Sixth and Main streets.

It is dangerous to cross the street there. Since school began on September 6, there have been two accidents there that have injured students. There have been several other near-misses.

In the winter it is already dark by the time we get to that crossing after school. There is a lot of traffic at those hours, too, because some people are driving home from work.

Often you have to try to run when there's not enough time. We would feel much safer if there were a light.

Name	Grade	Address	Phone

Speak Out

Our democratic system of government is an engine that runs on words. It sputters on through committees and hearings, speeches and testimony. To make it run your way, you have to add your voice to the fuel.

A speech makes you organize your thoughts and refine your arguments. It gives you a chance to have your views recorded in the minutes of public meetings and to get on mailing lists so you'll know of future activities. And people who care enough to speak about an issue in public command respect. "Whenever I get up to speak," says Alex Reinert, "I remind myself that it takes a lot of courage to get up in front of a group of strangers. Everyone knows that. So just getting up is impressive."

Here are some tips for making good speeches:

▲ Start by writing an outline of what you want to say.
■ Rehearse a lot. Practice on your parents, your friends, your plants, your dog, your mirror.
● Take your outline with you and refer to it if you need to when you speak. But try not to read it. Look at the people you want to convince.
▲ Smile. Try to have fun. You're not in a dentist's chair.
■ Begin by saying who you are and why you are there. Your personal experience is important. Then get right to the point. Say what you want and why you should get it. Keep your speech short.
● Bring things like photos, posters, or charts with you that will help make your point. Show them during your speech.
▲ If you get stuck, or if you don't like how you sound, stop, take a deep breath, and start again. People will understand. Everyone gets nervous.
■ If you are speaking into a microphone, try to keep your mouth about an inch away. Speak in a loud, clear voice.

USE THE MEDIA

TV and newspaper reporters are paid to come up with stories every day, even when there's nothing happening. *They need stories.* If you lay a story in their laps, a story about a confident and determined group of young people working skillfully to make an important change, chances are good you'll see yourselves on the TV news and in the next morning's paper.

But things can go wrong. Sometimes reporters arrive too early or too late or leave at the wrong time. They quote the wrong people or take a photo that doesn't show what you want. It turns out that getting publicity is easy. The challenging part is having them write the story you want.

You'll succeed if you can give reporters an exciting story with clear news hooks and things to photograph or film. In short, give them a story that practically writes itself, a story that you yourself would like to read. Here are some tips:

Get the reporter you want. Do a little digging into each station or paper. Who covers the appropriate subject, such as schools, the environment, or peace issues? Go to the library and read some of their stories. Do you like them? If not, is there a feature or general assignment reporter whose stories you like better? Call the station or paper and ask specifically for that person. Tell your story idea briefly, emphasizing the most interesting points.

Robyn Eliason (*speaking*) and other Bel Air School leaders speak to the press on the day after they were expelled from school for protesting against Styrofoam trays and plastic utensils. (See page 157 for their story.)

141

Write a press release. Use it to set up the story you want to see written. Put quotes in it, so you can state your position exactly the way you want to say it. Give it to reporters before your event, and have it ready to give them again during the event. Here's an example:

PRESS RELEASE

FOR IMMEDIATE RELEASE   Contact: Judy Dribble
                                           555-4431
                                           (after 4:00 P.M.)

Lincoln Students to Protest Sexism in Basketball Program

On December 16 at halftime of the Lincoln-Washington boys' basketball game, a group of students at Lincoln School will demonstrate to protest the inequality of the resources given to the boys' and girls' basketball programs. They will march around the court carrying signs of protest and singing a new song they have made up, ''Sweet Georgie Brown.''

''We have to wait until the boys are finished to practice,'' says Lisa VanDunk, a junior forward on the Lady Bulldogs. ''Some of us who live in the country don't get home until after nine.'' Girls also say that unlike the girls, the boys' team gets school laundry service, cheerleaders, and bus transportation to the games. ''It's just sexism,'' says guard Alice Press.

Girls say that they play their games after school on weeknights, when few people can attend, whereas the boys play on weekend evenings. The protest will also include boys who sympathize with the girls' complaints.

When: December 16, 1992
Where: Lincoln School Gym, 12 Maple Street, Sweetwater
           (rear entrance)

A press release should be designed to make it as easy as possible for a reporter to write the story you want written.

At an event or a press conference, use props. Try to think like a photographer: what prop would really dramatize, in a picture, what you want to say? When, at their first press conference, kids working on the Children's Peace Statue planted marigolds in the nose cone of an old missile, photographers loved it.

Decide in advance who will speak to the press. Assign that person to stay with reporters during the event.

Give another copy of the press release to reporters at your press conference. Don't assume they kept the one you sent them. Make their job as easy as possible.

Get started on time. Reporters usually want to cover the story, get back to the office, and write it up or edit video footage. Often they work on very tight deadlines. Help them by starting right on time.

Get to know reporters. Thank them. Send them updates. Think of ways to stay in touch. That way, the next time you need help, you'll know someone to call.

At an early press conference, a Kids' Committee member holds up a sign thanking a bank that let project members open a free account. Behind her is the nose cone from a missile.

ASK FOR MONEY AND OTHER SUPPORT

Linda Warsaw started Kids Against Crime in an office donated by the district attorney. It was filled with furniture donated by a store owner going out of business. The photocopy machine, the coffee machine, the notepads, and even the pencils were all donated. How did she manage it? "I asked for it," she says.

If your project is ambitious, sooner or later you will have to ask for help. You'll have to buy land or put on a food drive for a shelter or just buy stamps or pay for phone calls. Here are some ideas for raising money and resources:

Offer your talent, time, and energy for sale. Wash cars. Bake things. Make a tape of the songs you write — just like the kids of the Children's Rain Forest — and sell it.

Round up things and hold a yard sale or a garage sale.

Organize fund-raising events. Get a band to donate an evening and have a dance. Put on a charity basketball or softball game. Get a business to donate something special — in exchange for publicity — and raffle it off.

Ask businesses to give you things you need.

Go door-to-door and ask. Go in pairs or larger groups and in the daytime. Make sure someone knows your route. Stay on the porch unless you know and trust the person who opens the door.

Give your own money. Do like Justin Lebo, who challenged his parents to match every dollar he spent from his allowance to buy bike parts for needy kids. Or like Allison Steiglitz, of Miami, Florida, who used the money she was given for her bat mitzvah to buy food for people who couldn't leave their homes.

Most people hate to ask someone else for help. It makes them feel weak. If someone says no, they take it personally, as if it means they're no good. But as Linda Warsaw puts it, "Ask and you might get something. If you don't ask, you won't get anything." These ideas will help you feel more comfortable asking for help:

Look right at each person you're asking. Smile. Dress neatly (that doesn't have to mean expensively). Let your enthusiasm for your project show. Remember, you're offering someone a chance to be part of something very special.

Ask for only one, clear thing. Be able to say in a few words why you need help. Rehearse the asking sentence until you're comfortable. Suggest a specific donation. Two books. Ten dollars. A blanket.

After you have asked for something and said why you need it, don't say anything until they answer. Clamp your jaw shut no matter how badly you want to keep talking. You have to let the other person answer, even if it's to say no.

If the answer is no, listen hard to that no. Try to figure out where it's coming from. Do they need a little more information? Are they too busy right now to really listen? Are they giving you information about themselves that might help you present your idea a different way? See if you think the no contains a door for a yes or a maybe. Try one more time, or ask if there's a better time to talk. If that doesn't work, thank them politely and move on.

144

Consider making your group into a nonprofit corporation. If your group incorporates as a nonprofit, whoever gives you money can deduct the value of their donation from their taxes. That's a big advantage, especially to people who pay a lot of taxes. Incorporation also lets you ask for donations from corporations, foundations, and even the government.

You'll probably have to get a lawyer to help you become a corporation. And in most states, people younger than eighteen cannot be on the board of directors. So set up an adult board and a youth board, and make it clear in your incorporating papers that yours is to be a youth-directed group. Have the adults you trust the most handle the money. Once you've become a nonprofit corporation:

Choose your board of directors carefully. They make the important decisions for the group. Don't choose just your friends. Invite people to join the board — kids or adults — according to how much they can help and how hard they will work. Look for some people with specific skills you might need, like successful experience working with reporters or raising money.

Write out a one-page preliminary proposal for a grant, with a budget. Say who you are, describe your project, and give a list of the things you need and why. Say as precisely as you can how much each of the items will cost. The proposal gives you something basic to leave with every potential donor you meet.

Try to visit potential donors in person before writing lengthy, detailed proposals. Write them a letter and follow up with a call requesting a visit. Let them react to your ideas and contribute their own thoughts. With luck, they'll end up telling you exactly how to write a successful proposal for funding from them. And you'll have an insider friend.

During your visit, say exactly how much money you need and why. Don't go in saying, "We need a thousand dollars for our project." Say, "We need $1,100 for the cost of printing and mailing the next two issues of our newsletter. Here is a copy of our specific budget."

▲ ▲ ● ■ ■

"THE ADULTS HAVE HELPED US MAKE OUR DREAMS COME TRUE, BUT THE IDEALS AND GOALS ARE OURS."
— LINDA WARSAW, FOUNDER, KIDS AGAINST CRIME

■ ■ ● ■ ■

A nice-looking thank-you note, signed by members of your organization, always helps.

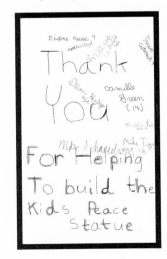

Research funding sources: corporations and government grants. Here are some good sources of information that should be at any big library.

For rich people:

▲ *Who's Wealthy in America.* This directory gives the names and addresses of about 50,000 millionaires, state by state.

◼ Annual reports of organizations that do things similar to what you do. They usually include a list of the major donors to the group.

● You can buy or trade lists of people who have given money to organizations like yours, or of subscribers to magazines related to your projects. Contact the organizations and magazines.

For foundations:

▲ *The Foundation Directory.* Look in the index for words like *Children, Youth, Environment,* or *Peace,* and then find the names of foundations that give to those areas. Each listing will tell you how and when to apply for grants.

For corporations:

◼ The law says that most corporations can give up to 10 percent of their pre-tax earnings to charitable causes, although unfortunately most give far less than that. Some corporations, like the Ronald McDonald Children's Fund, specialize in gifts to young people. The *Taft Corporate Giving Directory* includes comprehensive profiles of major corporate foundations and corporate charitable giving programs in the U.S.

For grants from the U.S. government:

● *The Catalogue of Federal Domestic Assistance,* published by the Government Printing Office.

Linda Warsaw: Young Fund-Raiser

Linda Warsaw, nineteen, has been fund-raising for Kids Against Crime since she was eleven. She says:

"Do research on the person you're going to meet before you visit. If you're about to ask the chief of police for office space, read up on recent cases. Say, 'You really did a good job on that kidnapping case.' A compliment never hurts if you mean it. That way the chief knows you know about him or her.

"Get to know the person while you're there. Tell them about yourself. Ask about them. Notice what's around the office. See if you can find clues about what they're interested in. You'll probably want to keep the relationship going after your visit.

"Tell people about your personal experiences in your presentations. I speak a lot to service clubs, like the Elks and the Eagles. They've all been burglarized. They understand how I felt when I was.

"Most of all, *try*. If they say no to the first thing you ask for, have something else in mind they can support."

BOYCOTT

Boycotting means not buying the products of companies that behave in ways you think are wrong. We've seen, for example, how a kid-led boycott of tuna companies helped force the companies to catch tuna in a way that spared dolphins.

American kids between the ages of four and twelve spend six *billion* dollars a year buying things. Teenagers spend even more. If you're going to make the people who run those companies rich, shouldn't you have a say in what the companies do?

Boycotts often go through stages. There's a lot of excitement and attention when you announce the boycott, and then nothing happens for a while. It's like you're in a submarine. You know the company's out there somewhere, but you don't know what they're thinking. Usually they're trying to wait you out. Many boycotters give up. Here are some tips so you won't:

Make sure the company is really doing something wrong. Do your research. Be fair. Don't punish a company unless there really is a problem.

Prepare for the long haul. Don't make your only strategy be a boycott. Combine it with other actions.

If you decide to boycott a big company, check to see whether anyone else is boycotting it. A good source of information about boycotting is the *Nation Boycott Newsletter*, which gives information about boycotts for human rights, peace, labor, animal rights, the environment, and other categories. To order, write Todd Putnam, 6506 28th Avenue NE, Seattle, WA 98115.

Consider keeping it local. You don't have to organize a big national boycott to attract attention. A well-directed local action can work very well.

Education is the key to success. In the Coke machine example above, the boycott organizers worked all year long to educate other students about why they were boycotting Coke. If they hadn't, very few students would have cared, and the action would have fizzled. How did they do it? "We

▲ ▲ ● ■■■■■

"BOYCOTTS LED BY CHILDREN REALLY WORK, BECAUSE EXECUTIVES KNOW THAT TODAY'S CHILDREN ARE TOMORROW'S CONSUMERS. THEY THINK IT'S IMPORTANT FOR THE COMPANY TO MAINTAIN A GOOD IMAGE WITH CHILDREN. AND ALREADY CHILDREN HAVE BEEN ABLE TO ALTER THEIR PARENTS' PURCHASING PATTERNS."
— TODD PUTNAM, EDITOR, *NATION BOYCOTT NEWSLETTER*

■■■■ ● ■ ■

wrote fact sheets," remembers Alex Reinert. "We sponsored the debate. We put articles in the school newspaper. We got permission to make presentations in each homeroom. We never stopped working at education."

Boycotting Locally to Attack a Global Problem

In 1987, students at Rindge and Latin High School in Cambridge, Massachusetts, believed that by doing business in South Africa, the Coca-Cola Company was supporting apartheid — a brutal system of racial separation. They decided to boycott Coke. But they didn't attack the whole company. They boycotted the Coke machine in the student center.

Their goal was to get the machine removed from the school. They knew the school administration would object, because the money from sales helped pay for the school's football program. The boycott lasted all year. By spring, sales at the machine dropped from two hundred cans a day to about twenty-five cans a month.

Newspaper stories reached executives at Coca-Cola's headquarters in Georgia. Coke sent a vice president all the way to Massachusetts to debate the daughter of a black South African leader at the school. Six hundred students watched, and then voted 70 to 30 percent to get rid of the machine.

Finally the administration hired a truck to haul the machine away. What did the students gain? "We got fifteen hundred people at our school to think and learn and consider an action about South Africa," says Alex Reinert, a boycott leader. "We came to feel that we had power in a situation where we had been told we were powerless."

LOBBY

Kids all over the country are convincing lawmakers to pass laws and use tax money to do such things as create parks, clean up poisonous waste sites, and help people without homes.

To change or make a law, or get public money spent on your project, you have to have your idea written up as a bill — a draft of a proposed law — and then guide it through the steps through which a bill becomes a law.

First you have to find a lawmaker to sponsor your bill, or be its main guardian in the legislature. The ideal sponsor is one who is both powerful — say the chairperson of a key committee in the legislature — and who believes in what you're trying to do. Of the two, the second is more important. Find someone who will really work with you.

To attract a lawmaker, you usually have to show three things:

▲ That your idea is important.
■ That a law is needed to make it happen.
● That there is something in it for the lawmaker, usually votes — from your parents, neighbors, or people in the community affected — or good publicity.

It pays to start early — three to six months before a legislative session. Lawmakers are busy. If you try to pop your idea on them during a session, you won't even get to meet them.

Once you have a sponsor, someone has to draft the bill. You should write it yourself, just the way you would want it, and give it to your sponsor. Then listen carefully and with an open mind to the changes she or he may suggest. You may have to compromise to help your sponsor succeed. *But never compromise away the heart of what you want.*

After your bill is drafted, it will be introduced into the legislature, that is, put on a schedule for action and then assigned to a committee, where a few lawmakers will look at it closely.

Now your job is to support your sponsor. Make it as

easy as possible for him or her to get your bill passed with as few changes as possible. Here are some things you can do:

Visit each committee member. Don't take much of their time. Say why you want the bill passed. Show your enthusiasm.

Try to find other groups that will support your bill. Maybe you can support a bill that *they* are trying to pass. Form partnerships of groups.

Write letters to legislators and to the governor or mayor. Let them know you exist and why what you want is important. To become law, your bill has to pass through three doors:

▲ *Committee referral.* The committee has to recommend that your bill get passed and send it to the legislature for a vote.

■ *A floor vote.* The whole legislature then has the opportunity to vote on your bill.

● *Executive signature.* If your bill is passed by the legislature, the governor or president then has to give it his or her approval by signing it into law.

Unexpected things tend to happen right at the end. Maybe the bill gets passed with no money. It gets stuck to another bill that doesn't have anything to do with yours. It gets changed. Your sponsor must know which changes are acceptable to you and which aren't. Again, it is better to let the bill die now and try again next session than to accept a compromise you don't want.

HELP ELECT WHOM YOU WANT

Even if you can't vote yet, you can have a say in who represents you. Here's how:

Pay attention to what elected officials do. Who is your mayor? Your governor? Who's on your school board? How did they get there? What do they believe in? What do they really want? What are they working on? You should know these things. Read the papers. Go see them. Ask them how they feel about the things you care about.

TEDDY ANDREWS, YOUTH COMMISSIONER

In 1989 Teddy Andrews, then eight years old, campaigned for Donald Jelinek, who was running for city council of Berkeley, California. Why? He liked Jelinek's politics. Jelinek seemed interested in the homeless. So was Teddy.

Teddy worked hard for his candidate. He went door-to-door, urging people to vote for Jelinek. He put up posters and did whatever else he was asked.

When Jelinek won, Teddy asked Jelenik to appoint him to the Berkeley Youth Commission. You didn't have to be twenty-one to serve, and it seemed to Teddy a way to get some things done. Jelinek said yes.

At the first meeting, Teddy showed up with a written agenda, a "wish list" for the homeless children of Berkeley. The list included paper, pencils, clothing, more school buses, and scholarship money. He also wanted a children's bathroom installed in a neighborhood park to keep kids safe from the drug dealers who hung around the outdoor bathrooms. Teddy has since helped to make some of those wishes on his list come true.

Work to elect good candidates and defeat bad ones. How? During election campaigns, show up at the office of a politician you care about and who will support your project. Stuff envelopes. Staple position papers together. Go door-to-door. Make yourself useful.

Get to know politicians personally. Go see them. Introduce yourself. Politicians are easy to meet when they're campaigning. Tell them about your project. Make sure they know what you want.

Raise and contribute money for good candidates. People younger than eighteen contributed 1.4 million dollars to federal candidates in the 1988 elections. The law says minors may contribute to political campaigns if they make their decisions "knowingly and voluntarily."

Expect politicians to pay you back. When your group needs something, go to the politicians you helped. Remind them that you worked for them. Tell them you expect their help.

OMAR CASTILLO: WALKING FOR THE RAIN FOREST

In the spring of 1987, nine-year-old Omar Castillo from Mexico City walked with his father nearly eight hundred miles to try to convince a governmental official to save the last rain forest in Mexico. The official patted him on the head and told him not to worry.

But Omar kept right on walking, to the palace of the president of Mexico. When the president wouldn't see him, Omar and his father set up a tent in the president's square. Every day, Omar marched around the square to protest the cutting of the forest. Each day, more and more children joined him, and on the fourth day the children's march attracted news reporters.

Finally the president was embarrassed into a meeting. He promised Omar that within a year the cutting would stop. A year later, he broke his promise.

Now Omar is thirteen and trying to organize children to save the forest. "All the children I have talked to are as determined as I am," he says. "If the grown-ups don't stop cutting, hundreds of thousands of children will have to go there and make a chain that will surround the forest! And we will not move until they stop logging."

PROTEST AND DEMONSTRATE

Chanting, marching, singing, picketing, protesting — these are the things people usually associate with causing change. But for the most part, people demonstrate when other ways have failed.

When to demonstrate:

▲ When you're not getting anywhere by less disruptive tactics. In other words, you've tried talking, and nobody's listening.

■ When there's no time to do anything else: they've just fired your teacher, the government has just sent troops for a cause you don't support, or a week from today, they plan to tear down a place of historical importance.

Here are some things to think about if you're organizing a demonstration:

What are your goals? To attract more attention? To cause a change in someone's position? To embarrass someone publicly into more reasonable behavior? Think carefully. Will a demonstration achieve your goal?

When will your demonstration be over? What needs to happen for you to stop demonstrating? In 1991, twenty members of the Environmental Youth Alliance in Victoria, British Columbia, went on a hunger strike for five days to protest plans to log a forest they loved. Nothing else had worked. They talked it over in advance and decided not to eat for five days. They arranged to have doctors monitor their health. They were prepared to suffer, but not to die, for the forest. This was an important, conscious decision, made *before* the demonstration. You should know, too, when you are prepared to stop.

How much risk are you willing to take? Getting laughed at? Being kicked out of school? Getting arrested? Getting hurt? Think out the consequences in advance. Think of the worst thing that could happen. Prepare and rehearse. Consult others who have done such things. Find out what went right and wrong. What would they do differently? Tell someone you trust what is going on and have them at the site or on call. Take some coins with you to the demonstration in case you need to call someone.

Be creative. Make it dramatic. During a ceremony at the United Nations for the Day of the Child, seventeen-year-old Kurtiz Schneid dressed in a clown suit as "Ronald McToxic" to draw attention to McDonald's use of polystyrene packaging (which they have since stopped). Speaking to the shocked U.N. delegates, he said, "Show your commitment. The planet deserves a break today."

If you're going to demonstrate, be like Kurtiz. Think of how you can dramatize the problem. Make up chants and songs, or make up new lyrics about your fight to old songs such as "We Shall Not Be Moved" or "We Shall Overcome." Make posters. Dress up. Have some fun. Be bold. Make it count.

You have a right to demonstrate. The Constitution guarantees it.

Don't worry about getting laughed at or ridiculed. Sometimes that shows you're being effective.

NEGOTIATE

If by some combination of these tools, by the clarity of your vision and the force of your energy, you have convinced whoever holds power to talk with you, hold the high fives a while longer. You still may have to negotiate, or bargain, with them to get what you really want. Here are some tips:

Before you negotiate, make sure you know what you really want. Now is the time to go back and look at the vision statement you wrote out at the beginning. That's the part you don't give away.

Have a specific goal in mind, but be flexible in how the goal is reached. Consider fallback positions. Is there anything else you'd settle for if you can't get what you absolutely want? Would you let them phase in your solution over a longer time? Would you help raise funds for it? Think carefully about what you might be able to give up without sacrificing what you really want.

▲ ▲ ● ■ ■

"CONGRESS SHALL MAKE NO LAW . . . ABRIDGING THE FREEDOM OF SPEECH, OR OF THE PRESS; OR THE RIGHT OF THE PEOPLE PEACEABLY TO ASSEMBLE."
— FROM THE FIRST AMENDMENT TO THE U.S. CONSTITUTION

■ ■ ● ■ ■

▲ ▲ ● ■ ■

"WHETHER IT IS STRIKES OR WAR, THE BIGGEST BATTLES IN HISTORY HAVE ENDED SITTING DOWN AT A TABLE."
— LECH WALESA

■ ■ ● ■ ■

Choose representatives carefully, and work with them closely. Make sure your representatives know exactly what your group will allow them to agree to. Expect them to come back to the group whenever there's an important new proposal on the table. Have people standing by to help. Your representative should never be embarrassed to say, "I need to talk with my group before I answer this."

Negotiate only with those who have enough power to do the things you want. Don't let them send you a go-between who has to ask someone else to make a decision. Insist on dealing with a decision maker.

Listen carefully to the other person. Try to understand what they really want and need. Sometimes they are saying one thing but their voice or the way they are acting tells you they really mean something different. Try to understand them. What are the attitudes that cause them to think as they do? Find out as much as you can about them before you start negotiating with them.

Make it easy for them to do what you want. Maybe they'd like to do it your way, but they don't want other adults to see them give in to kids. Can you help them? Show that you respect them personally and that you respect their authority. Keep the disagreements to the issues. Treat them as worthy opponents in a specific situation, not as enemies.

Try to be open about your own feelings when negotiating. If you're scared or nervous, there's no harm in letting it show. That doesn't make you weak.

Never let a deadline force you into making an uncomfortable decision. If this issue is truly important, there's always time to think carefully and get it right.

Write down the final agreement, and have everybody sign it. That way there's a record of what everyone agreed to. Make sure everyone gets a copy.

Don't worry too much about who gets credit. If it comes out the way you want, who cares who gets credit? When it's over, try to look for ways to be sincerely charitable toward the people you've just opposed.

▲ ▲ ● ■■■■

"THE BIGGEST HUMAN TEMPTATION IS TO SETTLE FOR TOO LITTLE."
— THOMAS MERTON

■■■■ ● ■ ■

156

USING THE TOOLS TOGETHER

The real power comes when you know how to use a whole set of tools together to fix something you know is badly broken or build something you really believe in.

One principle that often works is to move step-by-step up through the pathways that exist for making change, using approaches that increase in power and demonstrating and drawing attention to your cause only if everything else fails.

A good example happened in 1990, when a group of sixth-graders from the Bel Air Elementary School in Mounds View, Minnesota, caused their whole school system — thirteen schools — to switch from using plastics and Styrofoam in the lunchroom to buying dishwashers and using hard plates and utensils. They tried several ways to work with their teachers and school administrators until it became clear they weren't being taken seriously. Then they went outside the school to create pressure. That led to a settlement. Here's how they did it.

"IF THE ONLY TOOL IN YOUR TOOLBOX IS A HAMMER, ALL OF YOUR PROBLEMS WILL LOOK LIKE NAILS."
— FRIENDS COMMITTEE ON NATIONAL LEGISLATION

WORKING THROUGH EXISTING PATHWAYS AT SCHOOL

Just before the end of her fifth-grade year, Robyn Eliason asked her teacher if the school could get rewashable trays. He said no, that that would be impractical because the school would have to buy new kitchen equipment and hire new people to run the equipment, causing lunch prices to go up. "It seemed awful to me," Robyn says, "that the very people

157

who were teaching us about the damage CFCs [chlorofluo-rocarbons] were doing to the ozone and how fast landfills were being filled up were using Styrofoam in our own lunchroom."

In protest, Robyn and her friend Mitch Kauffman started bringing their own lunches to avoid eating off Styrofoam trays. No one seemed to care. "All that did was keep us from getting hot lunch," Robyn says.

In the fall of 1990, when sixth grade started, Mitch wrote a petition asking the school to replace the Styrofoam and plastic with hard, reusable trays, plates, and utensils. Robyn and Mitch got about 150 kids to sign it, educating them about CFCs and landfills as they asked for signatures.

They gave the petition to a school official and asked her to give copies to the school board and the principal. "That was probably a mistake," Robyn says. "We gave our only copy away. We should have made a bunch of copies and used them however we needed to. She could have just thrown it away and we would have had to start all over."

The school invited representatives from the Amoco Corporation, makers of the Styrofoam trays, to talk to a few selected students. The students prepared for a debate, learning all they could about alternatives to Styrofoam. They rehearsed and coordinated their questions. "It went badly from the start," Robyn recalls. "They treated us like infants. They gave us these ugly little rulers made of Styrofoam. Everybody just got mad."

After Amoco's visit, sixth-graders covered the halls with environmental posters. Students started bringing hard plates from home to avoid using the lunchroom's Styrofoam. "Almost the entire sixth grade did it for about a week until the principal said the plates were unsanitary and made us stop."

Fifteen sixth-graders attended the next meeting of the Mounds View school board. They coordinated their speeches to make sure each student said something a little different and to make sure that everyone stressed the main point — for the school to get hard, washable, reusable trays and utensils.

Robyn Eliason (*at microphone*) tells her school board why it should switch from Styrofoam trays to reusable plates.

"When we finished, the board members said, 'Oh, we're so glad you talked to us about this' and 'We'll set up a meeting to discuss this,' " Robyn recalls. "But basically they just dropped the whole issue when we went away."

CREATING PRESSURE

Tired of being treated lightly, thirty-five sixth-graders met on the playground at recess and decided to organize a demonstration. They would march into the lunchroom on the Monday after Earth Day, link arms, and chant. They would refuse to leave until the school would agree to discuss their concerns seriously. They would call reporters and try to get them to cover the event.

Six leaders emerged, and they divided up responsibilities. Talking on the school bus, on the phone at night, in the halls between classes and at recess, they planned the action, practiced chants, and made signs.

They decided to tell one teacher. "We all trusted her," Robyn says, "and we needed a place in the school to keep our protest signs, and we wanted her feedback. At first she said, 'Maybe you should try something else first.' But when we listed all the things we'd tried already, she said, 'Well, it's up to you.' She agreed to let us keep our signs in her classroom."

159

The night before the protest, Robyn and Mitch called TV stations in the Twin Cities area. "I called the main number and asked to talk to the newsroom, and they transferred me over to a reporter," Robyn says. "I explained what was going on and what we were going to do and when. I asked if they wanted to cover it. They said sure, they'd be there."

On the morning of the protest, the students discovered that the teachers knew about their demonstration. Each homeroom teacher tried to talk the students out of it, without offering a solution to their concerns. The students decided to go ahead with the protest. "At first it was scary, but then we thought, What are they going to do — kick us all out of school? There were thirty-five of us."

As reporters and photographers watched, the students started the protest at noontime. But just before the sit-in— the part the students wanted them to see the most — the news people suddenly left. "It was our first time with the press," Robyn says. "We didn't write a press release or give them anything to describe the protest."

After the reporters left, the teachers ordered the protesters to leave the lunch tables so that other kids could eat. The students marched to another part of the lunchroom, sat down on the floor, linked their arms together, and continued to chant. The acting principal ordered them back to their classrooms, threatening them with detention. Five kids left. She raised the threat to suspension from school. Thirteen more left. Seventeen remained on the floor, chanting. The teachers refused to negotiate with the students.

The teachers told the protesters they were suspended for two days. The students decided to clean up a local park the next day and invite reporters to watch them. Then they would hold a press conference.

At the park they explained to reporters that they had demonstrated only after many less disruptive tactics had failed. Holding up the bags full of trash they had gathered, they pointed out that they were dedicated environmentalists, not outlaws. Environmental activism was something that the school should reward, not punish, they said.

SETTLEMENT

A few weeks later, the school board met again to consider the matter. The favorable articles and news features about the students had created pressure on the school board. The sixth-graders had prepared to speak again, but before they could, the chairperson announced that the board had decided to install dishwashers in all thirteen schools of the Mounds View school system. "It isn't only that the school district can *teach* children," he told reporters. "We can learn from them, too."

Though they started with no experience, the sixth-graders succeeded in much the same way that many other activists have caused changes throughout history:

- ▲ Their tactics were based upon a single, important vision.
- ■ Their dedicated leaders communicated well with one another.
- ● They researched the facts, developed information of their own, and prepared carefully for events.
- ▲ They demonstrated their concerns effectively when left with no choice.

How did success feel? "It's a great feeling," says Robyn. "We did something really important for the school. We didn't just sit there and watch trash bags fill up with plastic and Styrofoam. I remember that at the beginning, everybody was thinking, What if it doesn't work? What if they punish us? Well, now I know that if you believe in something strongly enough, you can make things change. No matter what your age."

From *The Crane,* the
newsletter created by the
Children's Peace Statue
Kids' Committee.

RESOURCES

Here are some materials that will help you learn more about the stories, people, projects, and tools described in this book.

HISTORY

The information on apprentices given in the introduction came mainly from an essay by W. J. Rorabaugh called "A World Turned Upside Down: Apprentices, Masters and the Revolution." It will soon appear in a book titled *Beyond the American Revolution: Explorations in the History of American Radicalism*, edited by Alfred F. Young and published by Northern Illinois University Press, in DeKalb, Illinois.

The information about Charity Clarke and Anna Winslow came mostly from a book edited by Harriet Applewhite and Darlene Levy called *Women and Politics in the Age of the Democratic Revolution*. It was published in 1990 by the University of Michigan Press, in Ann Arbor.

The story of Harriet Hanson and the Lowell girls came from *A People's History of the United States*, by Howard Zinn. It was published in 1980 by Harper and Row, New York.

The story of the newsies comes from the book *Children of the City: At Work and at Play*, by Davis Nasaw. It was published in 1987 by Doubleday/Anchor of New York.

Several of the nine students who enrolled at Little Rock Central High tell their stories in *Voices of Freedom: An Oral History of the Civil Rights Movement from the 1950's through the 1980's*, by Henry Hampton and Steve Fayer. It was published in 1990 by Bantam Books of New York.

A very good story about the courage of young people in the civil rights movement is *Selma, Lord, Selma: Girlhood Memories of the Civil Rights Days*. It is about Sheeanne Webb and Rachel West, who as young girls marched from Selma to Montgomery, Alabama, for their rights. Their story was told to Frank Sikora in a book published by the University of Alabama Press, in Tuscaloosa, Alabama, in 1980. It may be ordered through the National Women's History Project, 7738 Bell Road, Windsor, CA 95492-8518.

Samantha Smith died, with her father, in a plane crash in 1985. But near the end of her life, she wrote a book worth reading called *Samantha Smith: Journey to the Soviet Union.* It was published by Little, Brown of Boston in 1985.

ABOUT TOOLS FOR CAUSING CHANGE

Organizing a social action project. For the past several years, the Giraffe Project has been trying to encourage citizenship, which they describe as "sticking your neck out," by publicizing local heroes. Aimed for college-age readers, *The Giraffe Project Handbook* helps describe how to set up a work plan based on a clear vision of what you want to accomplish. For ten dollars, it is available through the Giraffe Project, P.O. Box 759, Langley, WA 98260.

Interviewing people. A terrific example of what students can do with interviews is found in *Minds Stayed on Freedom,* by the youth of the Rural Organizing and Cultural Center. It was published by Westview Press of Boulder, Colorado, in 1991. A teacher's guide to what they did — which can easily be read by students, too — is in *Bloodlines: A Case Study of Educational Empowerment,* by Jay MacLeod. Contact the Rural Organizing and Cultural Center, 103 Swinney Lane, Lexington, MS 39035.

Using tools together. A newspaper called *The Practical Strategist* not only tells how to build a group that succeeds in causing good changes but also talks clearly about what can go wrong. It discusses why people lose confidence and why teams lose energy — and suggests what you can do about these problems. It is available through the Social Movement Empowerment Project, 721 Shrader Street, San Francisco, CA 94117.

GROUPS FOR YOU TO JOIN OR CONTACT

At the end of several of the chapters you read were the names and addresses of organizations you could join to do more. In the past few years, as problems have become identified and young people have become better organized, hundreds and hundreds of youth-centered organizations have sprung up. There are far too many to list here, but for a good guide to the groups, you can read the *Directory of American Youth Organizations,* available from Free Spirit Publishing, Inc., 400 First Avenue North, Suite 616, Minneapolis, MN 55401-1724.

A few especially effective groups are:

▲ Young and Teen Peacemakers, Inc., a grass-roots organization for kids eight to eighteen dedicated to youth empowerment, peace, and justice. They can be reached at: RD1, Box 171, W. Edmeston, NY 13485.

■ The Children's Music Network, a rapidly growing grass-roots organization of writers and performers of children's music, both kids and adults. P.O. Box 307, Montvale, NJ 07645.

● Concern About Kids' Environment (CAKE). Write to them in care of Freeport Middle School, Pleasant Street, Freeport, ME 04032, or, for younger kids, care of Mast Landing Elementary School, 116 Bow Street, Freeport, ME 04032.

▲ Kids Against Pollution, a national group of elementary school children with more than five hundred chapters in forty-two states. P.O. Box 775, Closter, NJ 07624.

■ Constitutional Rights Foundation, a large nonprofit Los Angeles–based organization "dedicated to educating young people to be more effective citizens." CRF provides teacher training assistance and curriculum materials that emphasize student interaction.

PHOTO CREDITS